REVISED EDITION

Preparing for Liturgy

A Theology and Spirituality

REVISED EDITION

Preparing
for Liturgy

A Theology and Spirituality

Austin Fleming

with Victoria M. Tufano

LTP

LITURGY
TRAINING
PUBLICATIONS

Acknowledgments

Scripture texts used in this work are taken from the New Revised Standard Version, © 1989, Division of Christian Education of the National Council of Churches of Christ of the United States of America (New York: Oxford University Press). Used with permission. All rights reserved.

Excerpts from the English translation of *The Roman Missal* © 1973, International Committee on English in the Liturgy, Inc. (ICEL); excerpts from the English translation of *Documents on the Liturgy, 1963–1979: Conciliar, Papal, and Curial Texts* © 1982, ICEL; excerpts from the English translation of *Rite of Christian Initiation of Adults* © 1985, ICEL. All rights reserved.

Excerpts from *The Taizé Office* © 1981, Les Presses de Taizé. Used by permission of GIA Publications, Inc., exclusive agent. All rights reserved.

"We Remember" by Marty Haugen. © 1980, GIA Publications, Inc., 7404 S. Mason St., Chicago IL 60638. All rights reserved.

"How Brightly Deep" or "The Call" by Suzanne Toolan. © 1971, GIA Publications, Inc., 7404 S. Mason St., Chicago IL 60638. All rights reserved.

"One Bread, One Body" by John Foley, SJ. © 1978, OCP Publications. All rights reserved.

This book was edited by Victoria M. Tufano and designed by Lisa Buckley. Audrey Novak Riley was the production editor, and Jim Mellody-Pizzato was the production artist. The cover photograph was taken by Antonio Pérez. The typefaces used are Sabon and Gill Sans. This book was printed by Bawden Printing in Eldridge, Iowa.

05 04 03 02 01 00 99 98   7 6 5 4 3 2

Copyright © 1997, Archdiocese of Chicago: Liturgy Training Publications, 1800 North Hermitage Avenue, Chicago IL 60622-1101; 1-800-933-1800; fax 1-800-933-7094; e-mail orders@ltp.org. All rights reserved.

Library of Congress Cataloging-in-Publications Data
Fleming, Austin.
    Preparing for liturgy : a theology and spirituality / Austin Fleming ; with Victoria M. Tufano.
        p. cm.
    Includes bibliographical references.
    1. Catholic Church — Liturgy. 2. Catholic Church — Doctrines.
    3. Spiritual life — Catholic Church. I. Tufano, Victoria M., 1952–. II. Title.
BX1970.F57   1997
264'.02 — cd21   97-14057
                                                                                      CIP

ISBN 1-56854-040-X
PREPAR

Contents

Foreword to the new edition **vi**

Chapter 1
Back to Basics **I**

Chapter 2
Let's Stop Planning Liturgies! **27**

Chapter 3
Speaking of Liturgy **38**

Chapter 4
Living the Tradition: A Contemporary Task **64**

Chapter 5
Negotiating the Rite **73**

Chapter 6
Spirituality and Liturgical Ministry **87**

Chapter 7
Reflections for Liturgical Ministers **I00**

Chapter 8
Blessing and Dismissal **I3I**

The work of liturgical reform seems to have no end — in part because in many places it seems that it has only recently begun! The renewal signaled by the promulgation of the *Constitution on the Sacred Liturgy* in 1963 had a rough beginning. Great changes were introduced too quickly and with scant preparation of the people. Inevitably, the church divided into two camps: those for and those against the changes in the Mass. Inadequate catechesis is to blame for many of the problems witnessed during the early renewal. Priests and people found themselves on choppy seas: Some were thrilled with the excitement of the adventure, and others were terrified that the ship of faith might founder. The waters have calmed and the ship is still afloat, but some ministers seem to be sailing without their charts.

The work of the liturgical renewal goes on in part because newcomers to the liturgical ministry want to learn, and in part because others have yet to learn the basic theology and spirituality that undergirds ritual prayer in our communion. This small book was first published in 1985, some 22 years into the present liturgical reform. It is a book for beginners — for those who are just starting and for those who want to begin again. I am gratified that over the past 12 years many have found it to be a helpful text in parish life, in college classrooms, in liturgy training programs and in workshops.

This revised edition with its new chapter comes with a new cover, but frankly, the material in these pages is as old as the hills. As I note in the conclusion: Anything here that seems to be new is only apparently so. At best these pages rehearse a theology, spirituality and liturgy as old as that upper room where Peter and John prepared for Christ's Passover meal. I make no apology for this; it is the way things are in the liturgical disciplines. We all need to regularly refresh our memory of the tradition we cherish. If we do not understand what is at the heart of our rites, then we are ill-prepared to minister these ancient mysteries in the sanctuary of God's people at prayer.

Even if the material here is old, I trust that its presentation remains fresh enough to interest both the newest people on the liturgy committee and pastors who have been presiding at Sunday eucharist since before the days of Vatican II. I especially hope that newcomers and old-timers might be able to sit down with this text and use it to come to some common understanding of what the church asks and expects of us in our worship today. Such dialogue, rooted in the tradition, the scriptures and the church's liturgical books, is precisely the kind of conversation we need to advance and deepen the work of the liturgical reform. Without it, we will be lost at sea.

I am grateful to Gabe Huck for trusting in the value of this text some 12 years after its original design. I am grateful to Victoria Tufano for her skill in helping to revise the larger text and in reorganizing some of the material.

— *Austin Fleming*

Chapter 1

BACK *to* BASICS

A five-year-old walked into the living room just as her parents' neighborhood Bible-study group completed its discussion of the images of Christ in the gospels of Matthew, Mark and Luke. The child asked the grown-ups what they had been talking about and was told, "We talked about God, sweetheart." The little one replied, "Who's God?" The silent tension in the room could only have been greater if the next question had been, "Where do babies come from?"

The simplest questions can be the most provocative, especially when posed by children. Perhaps this is why the youngest member of the Jewish family is the one who asks at the Passover table, "Why is this night different from all other nights?" There is a depth and honesty in a child's artlessness that disarms us. It cannot be dismissed as simplistic, and it will not be satisfied by complexities that evade the question.

The Passover meal provides a better environment for a child's query than did the Bible-study group in the story above. The adults in the study group had finished asking the questions, but the adults at the Passover table wait for the question to be asked again and again — from the guileless lips of a child.

We are invited to recapture both the bold innocence of children and the wisdom of those who seek to learn from their questions. The questions we are about to ask of worship are simple and provocative. These are questions we have asked before — and "answered" before. Our twofold purpose in posing them again is to see if we have become too easily contented with half-true or even false answers, and to delve once more into the mystery of those questions whose asking is ever the task of believers: Whom do we worship? Why do we worship? How do we worship?

Like the child's disarming question, these cannot be dismissed as simplistic, and they will not be satisfied by complexities that evade the question. We make our inquiry with a child's naïveté, hoping to disabuse ourselves of "adult" presumptions and preconceptions and to seek the answers with depth and honesty.

WHOM DO WE WORSHIP?

Whom do we worship? We worship God. The Christian expands this simple answer with a profession of faith: We show religious devotion and reverence in a service or rite; in prayer, we adore and venerate God as the One who creates, redeems and sustains all that is. Worship, therefore, is directed toward and offered to — is for — God.

The preposition *for,* in the last sentence, is significant and deserving of further reflection. If worship is for God, where do we, the worshipers, fit in this scheme of holy things? Is it not also true that worship is for those who offer it? An analogy with the rites surrounding death and burial may be helpful. Are the wake vigil, the processions, the funeral liturgy, the committal and the other ritual moments in the *Order of Christian Funerals* for the deceased or for the surviving community of believers? The Christian answers that such ritual is for both the faithful one departed and the faithful ones remaining. "But we do not want you to be uninformed, brothers and sisters, about those who have died, so that you do not grieve as others do who have no hope. For since we believe that Jesus died and rose again, even so, through Jesus, God will bring with him those who have died" (1 Thessalonians 4:13 – 14).

The community gathers to pray for God's bringing forth of the deceased into eternal life, and in doing so we pray for the dead. In praying for the dead we console one another with this message: Both in life and in death we are the Lord's (1 Thessalonians 4:17, Romans 14:8). Thus, our prayer is for ourselves, too. Prayer, then, has many dimensions and many effects; it benefits both those who pray and those on whose behalf we pray.

With this in mind, we return to our question: If worship is for God, can it also be for those who worship? The distinction is not mere semantic quibbling. When our ancestors in the faith failed to appreciate the difference, when they forgot that worship was for God and decided to get what they wanted from worship, they fashioned a golden idol for themselves. The distinction is the difference between worship and the potential for idolatry. The temptation to miss the difference is still with us and is one into which we pray not to be led.

Before the Council

For hundreds of years before the reforms of the Second Vatican Council,[1] even the casual bystander at Mass in a Roman Catholic church would have concluded that worship was for God: The Sunday morning gathering of hundreds of people kneeling in silent prayer until a ringing bell announced the entrance of priest and servers in the sanctuary created an ambience that directed attention away from ourselves and toward that central figure behind the altar rail—*alter Christus*—whose ministry it was to offer the holy sacrifice. This he did not so much with his back to the people, but facing the reserved sacrament in the tabernacle, from which store the faithful (a few of them) would receive the eucharist. Those who followed along in their English missals would be aware of these significant words in the Roman Canon: "Almighty God, we pray that your angel may take this sacrifice to your altar in heaven" (Eucharistic Prayer I). The priest prayed these words quietly in Latin, with head bowed and hands joined. The incense, ceremony and haunting chants of what we called "High Mass" served to heighten our appreciation that what we were doing, we were doing for God.

Such worship is no longer normative in the Roman rite. We have begun to restore our worship so that texts and rites might "express more clearly the holy things they signify [and that] the Christian people, as far as is possible, should be able to understand them easily and to take part in them in a celebration which is full, active, and the community's own."[2]

There is a tendency for some of us to look down our noses at the preconciliar liturgy and to pat ourselves on the back for what we have done to reform it. We easily forget that these older forms of praise were the faith expressions of our forebears whose fidelity to Christ's command, "Do this in memory of me," preserved for our own generation the meal and message of the new covenant. Others of us mourn the passing of the old forms, declaring that the changes following the Council destroyed the "true Mass" — often remembered through a veil of nostalgic reverie — and the church with it. We easily discount the faithfulness of the reformers. Worship, be it the model given to us by Trent or by Vatican II, always runs the risk of becoming an idol, an end unto itself.

Whom do we worship? Is worship for God or for us, or for both? The response is a sobering reflection away from us.

No More Prayer!

Suppose that for some strange reason, Christians around the world stopped praying tomorrow: no more private prayer, no more public prayer, no more hymn-singing, no more sacraments, no more prayer groups or Bible-study groups, no more preaching, no more worship.

Would God be any less for all this? Would God begin to pine for the days when heaven was stormed with prayer and thanksgiving? Would God feel empty or lonely?

The answer to all three questions is a disquieting "No." There is nothing that we are, nothing that we have and nothing that we can do for which God has a need. Nothing.

God does not need us. In fact, God has never needed us. God did not need the first man and woman in Eden, but God created them anyway. God had no need of the rest of creation either, but chose to create the world purely out of love. The God whom we worship needs neither us nor our prayer.

This is good news! Suppose that God did need something from us. What could we offer? All that we have and all that we are is already God's gift to us. The best we can do is to rewrap God's gifts to us and present them to their, and our, Creator as though they were from us. It's one thing to rewrap the gift your Uncle Harry sent you for Christmas last year and to give it to your neighbor this year. It's another thing altogether to send the rewrapped present back to Uncle Harry for his birthday! What Uncle Harry would find insulting, the Creator finds delightful.

> All-powerful and ever-living God,
> we do well always and everywhere to give you thanks.
> You have no need of our praise,
> yet our desire to thank you is itself your gift.
> Our prayer of thanksgiving adds nothing to your greatness,
> but makes us grow in your grace.
>
> (Preface for weekdays IV)

"Our desire to thank you is itself your gift" to us. Isn't that strange? God, who has no need of our prayer, puts within us the desire to worship. Should we conclude, then, that worship is for us? Our response here cannot be without some subtlety and ambiguity: All of our worship is given to God, who has no need of it but who does accept it. We offer that worship precisely because it is "our duty and our salvation" to do so.

We have stumbled upon the second of our "back to basics" questions: "Why do we worship?" Because the three questions are intimately connected, we will need to look at this "why" of worship before drawing out the implications of the sobering assertion that God has no need of our prayer.

Consider the difference between these two statements:

1. It is April 14 and I need to pay my taxes.
2. It is April 14 and I have a need to make a contribution to the Internal Revenue Service; I will pay my taxes.

The first statement expresses a sense of duty, obligation and imposed expectations; the second expresses a desire, a felt need, which may or may not be linked with external pressures. In order to understand why we worship (that it is our duty and our salvation), we first must acknowledge that God has no need of our worship. To understand further the "why" of worship we must investigate what kind of need prompts the worship we offer.

Our need to worship may stem from internal desire (God's gift to us) or from external obligation (as announced by scripture, church ordinance, family or peer pressure). Do some people have one kind of need and other people the other? No, we all have both. Regardless of our openness to it, God is always planting within us the desire to pray and offer worship. In addition, there is always set before the believing community the stated obligation to worship, which is ours by baptism and membership in the church. In this way, one sees that external obligation is more support than hindrance in our freedom to respond to God's activity in our lives. To give God "thanks and praise, always and everywhere" is our duty and our salvation— whether we feel it or not, whether we feel like it or not.

Why We Worship

Our need to worship rises out of that God-given desire that is the Creator's gift to us and is supported by that community of believers whose structure and faith announce that worship is our duty and our salvation. Our salvation rests in praising and thanking God, who has no need of our praise and thanks. This is why we worship: God made us, God loves us (even in our sin) and God saves us. To put it simply, God has done a lot for us, and we are in debt to God up to our ears! The debt is even greater than simply what we owe our saving God for our redemption. Jesus, in the Easter mystery of his dying and rising, has paid the debt for us. We owe a debt to God — and we owe God for letting the debt be written off in the gift of Christ's life for us.

How do we pay back a debt when the one we owe has canceled the debt? We don't, because we can't, but we ought to be deeply thankful and filled with praise for the one we owe. That's the way it is between God and us — whether we like it or not, whether we feel like it or not.

In this relationship there are significant inequalities — not all the parties are equal. We, the children of creation, are equal in that we all owe God a debt of thanks and praise, that is, worship. The inequality is that we are creatures and not the Creator; God made us and not we God. In this relationship we stand poor, with empty hands, before God, who fills our emptiness with love, mercy and life (which on our own we do not deserve, cannot earn and cannot fully return). God fills our emptiness with that which satisfies the greatest need of every human heart.

The inequalities of this relationship sometimes gall us. Like our first parents in the garden, we often succumb to the temptation to "be like gods." The result is that we end up in the foliage, concealing what has been revealed. We hear that voice at the breezy time of the day calling, "Where are you? Who told you that you were naked?" Clutching a few hastily gathered leaves to ourselves, we venture out in our nakedness to stand in the presence of our Creator. What can be our response but a plea for forgiveness and a pledge of praise and thanksgiving when we are pardoned?

Why do we worship? Because worship is of the order of things as it will be in the reign of God, where the original order of creation will be fully restored. We worship because worship is the most honest statement we can make about ourselves and the world in which we live.

Worship Is for God

Worship is the most legitimate and consummating of all human activities. It is the process of recognizing the right relationship of God with creation. Worship acknowledges debts owed and paid; the acknowledgment is expressed in praise and thanksgiving. Clearly, worship is God-centered and God-directed. This, however, does not deny that we who worship enjoy some benefit from the worship we offer. This mutuality is the stuff of covenant revealed in scripture.

That Was a Great Liturgy!

"That was a great liturgy!" How often have we made such a comment as we leave worship? How often has it been addressed as praise to those who prepare for and minister within the liturgy? What does this comment reveal about how we understand for whom the liturgy is offered?

That was a great liturgy! Is this another way of saying, "Well! We did a good job today of paying back the debt that can't be paid!"? Usually not. In some instances, "great liturgy" may simply indicate that the service did not leave those in attendance bored or disappointed. More often, though, a "great liturgy" is one that touches us, draws us in, speaks to us and makes us feel good. Our response to the question, "What makes a great liturgy?" may tell us more than we care to know about ourselves at prayer. Do we come to worship for God or for ourselves? Is the quality of worship determined by what it did for us aesthetically, or by what we did for God? The ideal, of course, is that in doing something for God we are rendered and surrendered closer to the Lord whom we came to serve.

Entangled in the Mystery

Christian worship is born of the divine humanity of Christ, the mystery that we name the Incarnation, the enfleshment, of God's Word. We, the community of believers, are forever entangled in this mystery. This is never more poignant and real than when we gather to offer "divine service," the liturgy. For Christians it is never a question of "for God or for us"; such distinctions are simply false in the light of the gospel. Worship is for God because God is for us; worship is for us because we are made for God. This is like the chicken-and-egg dilemma, where the answer to "which comes first" is "God, who made the chickens who lay the eggs." God enjoys a priority in the covenant relationship, a priority that surrendered itself to us in the mystery of Jesus' life, death and resurrection — the Paschal Mystery. This surrender was for us so that we might know again and forever the saving mercy of the God who made us.

Worship is where human beings experience in a unique way the divine and the truly human. We need worship because it is the way for us to experience all that is good and holy. "All that is good and holy," however, does not need to experience what is human and imperfect; much less does God need our liturgy for such an experience of human imperfection.

If worship leaves us untouched, it has failed. If, however, the liturgy touches us but does not lead us to experience the God we worship, then it has doubly failed, for it has left us self-satisfied and self-interested. Self-satisfaction and self-interest are the fruit of the tree that grew in the middle of that ancient garden; this fruit sometimes looks suspiciously like a golden calf.

Worship and Idolatry

We are tracing here the sometimes fine line between worship of God and idolatry. This is not to suggest that idols have been crafted and set up for worship in our churches. It is simply to remind us that idolatry is not a thing of the past, and to help us see that the worship itself can become an idol. Perhaps our greatest temptation to idolatry is the temptation to "worship" our own worship, to make it an end in itself. It is our task to preserve the liturgy as a treasure that has been handed down to us, but when such preservation becomes its own reward, the liturgy becomes a thing, an object. Because we who prepare the liturgy are appropriately enmeshed in it, we must always be careful that our worship does not become an image of ourselves. The liturgy is an icon of the Lord's saving mystery in which we surely see our own redeemed reflection, but it must never become a vanity mirror. "Mirror, mirror, on the wall, whose liturgy is fairest of them all?"

When our worship leads us to God, it has about it a fullness, depth and vitality with which nothing can compare. Worship that leads us back to ourselves, however, is a dead end where the worshipers are left to battle out their petty differences in a spirit that is often less than holy. Wisdom lies in knowing the difference and praying accordingly.

Priestly People or Pawns

At first glance, what we have said thus far may appear to reduce the role of worshipers to the status of pawns, and in any but the Christian scheme of things this would be a valid critique; but we are the baptized, and this makes all the difference. The American bishops have put this in beautiful perspective:

> The most powerful experience of the sacred is found in the celebration and in the persons celebrating, that is, it is found in the action of the assembly; the living words, the living gestures, the living sacrifice, the living meal. [3]

This notion of the primacy of the assembly is not contrary to what we have already stated. We simply need to pay attention to four significant words in the quote from the document: *experience of the sacred.*

The sacred is revealed and experienced in the assembly and its actions. We are the body of Christ: the priestly, royal and prophetic community that embodies the Risen Lord in its prayer and work. We come to know who we are and what we are called to do by looking upon the face of God made flesh in Jesus, who is the Lord. The reflection we see is that of the redeemed sinner.

The worship community that honestly acknowledges the fullness of this reflection, that names its own sin and knows it is forgiven in Christ, is the community that meets and celebrates the Lord's mystery in its daily life outside the sanctuary.

The community that acknowledges only half of the reflection will be confused by faults in its redeemed self-image or left hopeless in the face of its own sinfulness. The former will be tempted to correct the faults by trying to "perfect" its ritual mirror, the liturgy; the latter will be tempted to wallow in self-pity, a form of self-centeredness alien to the liturgy. In each case, the sanctuary becomes a false center in the community's life where either the worship or the worshipers become the focus of attention. The idol here is not a golden calf but rather the self, created in its own, not God's, image.

New Boundaries

As liturgist Aidan Kavanagh has put it, "When altars become the center of the world, they skid to its edge." The true sanctuary of liturgy is the one that recognizes the world as the sanctuary of creation and redemption. The community that acknowledges its sin understands the sanctuary of liturgy to be a refuge, not an escape, for sinners; the community that rejoices in its redemption in Christ is eager to depart the sanctuary of liturgy to proclaim what it has celebrated there. Disciples of the Lord and the gospel know that in Christ the old, and potentially idolatrous, boundaries of God's sanctuary have been radically revised. Sanctuary is no longer the safe place we might imagine it to be. It is where we stand most naked before the Creator; it is where we find ourselves to be most vulnerable.

Whom do we worship? We worship God. Why do we worship? Because God is who God is (the name God revealed to Moses means "I AM WHO AM"). And because we are who we are, worship is for us, too. Thank God!

HOW DO WE WORSHIP?

How do we worship? We worship God through, with and in Jesus Christ. The opening words of each preface in the missal remind us:

Father, it is our duty and our salvation always and
everywhere to give you thanks through your beloved Son,
Jesus Christ.

That Christ is the mediator of the relationship between
God and humankind is clear from the central message of the
gospels: "The reign of God is at hand! Repent; turn your hearts
to God! I have come to announce my Father's mercy and to
show you the way home to God whose prodigal love is for all.
The way home is the way of the cross: I will walk it for you;
come, follow me!"

We Do Not Worship Jesus

Jesus is the announcement and the incarnation of God's reign
of mercy in our midst. This mercy is most clearly proclaimed
in the dying and rising of Christ, the first fruits of the new creation, in whom the debt of our sin is paid. Ours, now, is the
debt of praise and thanksgiving to the Father as we make our
way along the path of Jesus.

Jesus is not the object of our worship. Rather, Jesus came
to show us how to worship. That is why public prayer (with
only rare exceptions) is addressed not to Jesus but to the One
whose mercy Jesus reveals. Neither is Jesus simply a tour
guide on the way home. Jesus is the way home and is the channel of God's mercy upon us.

> Christ Jesus, high priest of the new and eternal covenant, tak-
> ing human nature, introduced into this earthly exile that hymn
> which is sung throughout all ages in the realms above. He
> joins the entire community of humankind to himself associat-
> ing it with himself in singing his divine song of praise.[4]

We pray by riding on the coattails of Jesus, whose sacrifice
makes him *the* priest, *the* liturgist, of the new covenant, the one
who has offered the perfect sacrifice once and for all. Jesus
is the one who sings eternally before the Creator the acceptable
canticle of divine praise. We worship by joining in the eternal
liturgy that Jesus offers. We join in that canticle of praise and

thanksgiving offered by the one who sang from the cross, "Father, into your hands I commend my spirit." We worship through Jesus because Christ is the most honest statement made about humankind. The prayer of Jesus is always heard, as is the prayer of those who worship through Christ, with Christ and in Christ.

Ritual and Our Prayer through Christ

If God has no need of our worship, then certainly God has no interest in the seasonal colors of vestments, whether altar servers will grow up to be women or men, or whether the assembly gathers in Sunday best or Saturday casual. None of this could possibly make any difference to God. Jesus, who is the revelation of God in our midst, was equally unconcerned with such matters. Most of the rules and guidelines by which we celebrate our public prayer are meaningless in God's eyes— Jesus would be among the first to disregard them, as the gospel accounts indicate. Yet what is meaningless in God's eyes is filled with importance for us, sometimes in healthy ways and sometimes not. Our respect and reverence for the rules and customs associated with our worship are important because they are concerned with *ritual*.

A good friend of mine often answers the question, "What's new?" with "Not much; just the ritual." He is imply-ing that life of late has been routine and perhaps even boring. Though this is a common enough understanding of the word, it is one of which we need to disabuse ourselves when speaking of worship. (It would be interesting to trace how the word "ritual" came to connote "rote and commonplace.")

I offer this definition of ritual:

Ritual is the community's experience of its belief. Ritual is the community's familiar, commonly accepted, inherited pat-tern of interaction with others as that community stands before God. Ritual rehearses the story of the community's ori-gins; thus it helps us know who we are. In ritual activity the divine is revealed in the ordinary, disclosing the value, meaning and purpose of the world and its people. The ritual moment celebrates the true order of things and preserves us from the threat of chaos.

If we ponder this definition, we may come to a deeper understanding of the turmoil, confusion and anger brought about by the nearly overnight changes in our liturgy in the 1960s. The havoc wrought in our worship spaces still reverberates. If ritual is our refuge from chaos, then tampering with that ritual can have chaotic repercussions.

Ritual and Roots

Ritual tells the story of our roots. It protects us from amnesia as it helps us keep alive the memory of how we came to be the people we are. Perhaps the only meaningless ritual is one that does not tell some people's story. Ritual activity locates us in the world; it roots us in the ritualizing community and provides us a home. Ritual bonds the individual to the community, preventing aimless wandering; it helps us know who we are in relation to others and the world. Membership in the ritual community preserves us from the ultimate, radical identity crisis.

Religious ritual — all true ritual has about it a religious character — is the patterned way in which the community stands before God. It is the time-tested path, the community's admittance to the holy ground. It is the sanctuary where Creator and creation meet, where the community looks upon the face of God and does not die. It is a particular moment of revelation in which the community experiences the story of its belief. In the telling and the doing of this story, the community meets its source and sustenance.

Remembering and Meeting

It was the day of my grandparents' fiftieth wedding anniversary. The celebration began with a festive eucharist and concluded with a reception and dinner.

After the party I asked my grandfather what had been the best part of the day for him. At first, he was hard put to single out just one moment, but at my insistence he finally admitted that a particular experience was staying with him. He told me that much of the day had been passed in recounting with friends and family the old stories that had been in the telling for over fifty years. Some stories were remembered easily, others nearly forgotten but quickly recalled. He said that this had been the heart of the day for him and then offered a gem of grandfatherly wisdom: "You know, when I hear those stories again, it's as if what is past is right here in front of me. It's mysterious."

My grandfather was of French Canadian descent, but his comment reflects the Hebrew proverb, "Remembering is a form of meeting." It is interesting that when families gather at Christmas, Thanksgiving, funerals, weddings and reunions, their principal activities are eating and storytelling. Also notable is that most families carry out these two activities according to some familiar, commonly accepted, inherited pattern of interaction. This is why a stranger invited into such gatherings feels "not at home." No matter how warm and sincere the invitation, the guest knows that he or she is not part of the family and the business of its gathering. To meet what is remembered and to take a rightful seat at the feast of that remembrance means that the individual must know well, and have a part in, the story told.

Ritual and Experience

If there has been some question of what these stories of family gatherings have to do with our prayer through, with and in Christ, the last paragraph should hint at some implications. Christian ritual is the church's familiar, commonly accepted, inherited pattern of interaction as it stands before God. It is the way we tell and do the story of our origins, remembering how we came to be who we are. In Christian ritual activity, the divine is revealed in the ordinary—the people, their bread and wine, water and oil, the spoken word, the laying on of hands—disclosing the value, meaning and purpose of the world and of those who live in it. Christian ritual names the true order of things and fortifies us against the chaos of sin. Our ritual prayer is an experience of who and what we believe.

In the assembly's ritual we tell again and again the story of our roots as God's people. Never is this telling more complete and articulate than in the celebration of the Paschal Triduum, the three days from the evening of Holy Thursday through Good Friday and the Easter Vigil to the evening of Easter day. This great three-day feast is the ritual moment for the family of believers, for in it we participate in the whole story of our salvation. It is most fitting that the climax of the feast, the Easter Vigil, is the perfect occasion for baptizing new members into their part in the story and their place at the table of remembrance. It is most appropriate that the new members of the family, the newly baptized, share the communion of the eucharistic table only after they have heard the family story in the Vigil's great liturgy of the word.

Ritual and Time

If the Paschal Triduum is the great annual Christian ritual, then the Sunday assembly for eucharist is the weekly remembrance of the Easter mystery. We gather on the Lord's day not only to tell but also to do the story of salvation. The doing of the story is our offering of praise and thanksgiving through, with and in Christ. The form of this doing is our prayer and gesture over bread and wine: taking, blessing, breaking and giving. All this we do at the Lord's command: "Do this in memory of me." In the eucharist we meet the One we remember. The Lord is with us! In our ritual we experience what we believe: The kingdom is, indeed, at hand. Emmanuel is God-with-us.

In all this we do not reenact the story of salvation. The saving events of the mystery of Jesus happened once, for all people and for all time. We do not somehow restage these events; we remember them. But our meeting the Lord in our remembering is not dependent on our memory or imagination. What we remember is the new covenant sealed in the blood of Christ. This sealing is the guarantee of divine encounter in the remembering by those who are incorporated by baptism into the story of the saving mystery.

The eucharistic feast of remembrance and meeting, however, is not confined to our present encounter with the mystery remembered. The ritual of the eucharist is one of realized promise: We experience a true glimpse of the great banquet in God's reign, where the feasting never ends; where the burdens of the past, the cares of the moment and the fear for the future are subsumed in the unending peace of God's presence. The ritual table of Sunday is the promise of home eternal; thus, the past remembered and the future hoped for are met in the now. Ritual provides our roots; it is equally our strength for the unknown mystery of tomorrow. As much as ritual provides our roots and the identity which flows from them, it equally serves as an articulation of what we are yet to become. The fruit of our ritual is strength for the already and yet-to-be-revealed mystery of God, who is our future. Of all this we can be sure, because the Lord whom we encounter is God who is, who was and ever will be.

Given all that we have said of ritual, we should not be surprised that there are so many laws and customs to protect our ritual activity. Tampering with such ritual has the potential of wreaking havoc in the life of the community. We are dealing with those familiar, commonly accepted, inherited patterns of interaction that are the community's path and admittance to the holy ground of encounter with God. The value of the laws and customs that surround our ritual is not inherent in the regulations themselves. Rather, their value lies in what they protect: the encounter of God and God's people at a common table for the telling of the story of creation, chaos and re-creation.

Breaking the Rules

There's no denying it: Jesus was the consummate rule-breaker. That's why the religious leaders were always after him. He broke the ritual rules. His greatest ritual crime is reported in the indictment: "This fellow welcomes sinners and eats with them" (Luke 15:3). Jesus supped regularly with the "unclean": tax collectors, prostitutes, lepers and outcasts. To add insult to injury, Jesus went about saying, "Truly I tell you, tax collectors and prostitutes are going into the kingdom of God ahead of you" (Matthew 21:31). In other words, the Gentiles and the unclean are coming home to God while you who so scrupulously keep the law are headed for condemnation.

It was not to gratify some delinquent or capricious spirit that Jesus broke the rules, but rather to establish the new ritual, the new covenant sacrifice sealed in the blood of the Lamb of God who takes away—cancels the debt of—the sin of the world. This new covenant in Christ's blood is for everyone, and particularly for those the old law deemed unclean and sinners.

We who worship through Christ are called to continue in this rule-breaking tradition: to break all the rules that protect us from serving one another, all the rules that divide rather than unite us, all the rules that keep "them," whoever they are, "in their place." Jesus would break every rule that leads us to believe that "they" are unclean and we are "saved." Most of all, Jesus would condemn whatever leads us to believe that participation in the ritual is all that is asked of us.

The New Ritual in Christ's Blood

"Do this in memory of me." These are perhaps the least understood of all Christ's words. We are quick to see that we are to continue to celebrate that upper-room supper at his bidding; we are slow to recognize that to "do this" in Christ's memory is to break and pour out ourselves for others in fulfillment of the demands of the new covenant. If we want to know the answer to the question, "How do we worship?" then we should be prepared for a sobering response. Our worship through, with and in the dying and rising of Jesus is never limited to the sacramentalizing of this mystery at the table of family stories. It means living out what we ritualize at table. Saint Paul writes with discomforting clarity on this point:

For as often as you eat this bread and drink the cup, you proclaim the Lord's death until he comes. Whoever, therefore,
eats the bread or drinks the cup of the Lord in an unworthy
manner will be answerable for the body and blood of the
Lord. Examine yourselves, and only then eat of the bread and
drink of the cup. For all who eat and drink without discerning the body, eat and drink judgment against themselves.

(1 Corinthians 11:26–29)

Ritual and Judgment

Insofar as we are becoming and living what we eat and drink,
we eat the Lord's supper worthily, but when the ritual moment
of eucharist becomes an end in itself, not leading us beyond
the table to break and pour out our lives in his memory, then we
eat and drink a judgment upon ourselves. Having referred to
ritual as our path and admittance to the holy ground of
encounter with God, we need to remember now that in the
gospel dispensation, the ground of divine encounter is the
whole of creation. What we do in the defined sanctuary of worship's duty is not an activity confined to that sanctuary, but
one whose field is the world. At the same time, the story we
tell and the ritual gestures we make are ours not simply because
they are the church's familiar and inherited patterns of interaction, but because we have become that story and have become
those gestures (which are the Lord's!) in our baptismal dying
and rising with Christ. In the gospel dispensation, the baptized
assembly and all its members are the living rituals of what
and who we celebrate: redemption through, with and in Christ
Jesus. Creation is our sanctuary, and our baptized lives are
its ritual.

Paul reminds us that those who eat and drink "without
discerning the body" eat and drink a judgment on themselves
(1 Corinthians 11:29). Scripture scholars help us to understand
body here as referring to the church, the body of Christ.
Certainly Paul's holy indignation over what has been reported
to him with regard to the Corinthians' gatherings — "One goes

hungry and another becomes drunk. . . . Do you show contempt for the church of God and humiliate those who have nothing?" (1 Corinthians 11:21–22)—justifies this interpretation. In other words: We do not eat the Lord's supper worthily if we do not recognize the Lord's body in our brothers and sisters away from the communion of that table. John's first epistle sums it up: Those who say their love is fixed on God, yet hate their neighbors, are liars. If we have no love for our brothers and sisters whom we have seen, we cannot love God whom we have not seen (see 1 John 4:20).

How Do We Worship?

We worship through, with and in Christ the Lord. Christ is the way, and there is no other. It was the sacrificial Lamb of the Cross whom the Father received, and it is the Lamb's victorious hymn of praise that the Father hears. Christ's sacrifice was once, for all; the sacrifice we offer is one of praise and thanksgiving as a memorial, a remembering, of Jesus' dying and rising. Our sacrifice is Christ's, for it is a share in the *sacrificium laudis* (sacrifice of praise) that Christ continually offers before the Father in that sanctuary which has no end.

Having seen that the whole of creation is our sanctuary and that our baptized lives are its ritual, we can better understand how our offering of thanks and praise is our duty and our salvation. Our duty does not end and our salvation is not accomplished simply by our share in worship's ritual, but rather, by how our prayer together in Christ is an icon of our life together in Christ, and for the world. This is why we are able to say that Jesus the rule-breaker would reject whatever leads us to believe that participation in the sanctuary ritual is all that is required of us. With Christ, we make the same rejection when we pray that it is our duty and our salvation always and everywhere to give thanks and praise. Those who ponder the relationship between liturgy and social justice will find in these words the solid link that makes the two a unity.

Summing Up

Our worship as Christians is the gathering of the redeemed sinful on God's holy ground. The joy of this gathering is that we who come empty-handed, offering a prayer that God does not need, are welcomed and heard because our path and admittance to this holy time and place is Christ, our brother and Redeemer. The familiar, commonly accepted, inherited pattern of this sacred encounter and celebration is the dying and rising of Jesus. We live by our share in the One whose life was broken and poured out for our sake so that we might give of our broken and healed selves for the life of the world. The ritual moment of this encounter anchors us in the embrace of God's loving and merciful arms, where we are truly at home, so that we might live what we have celebrated, now in the meeting tent of the whole of creation.

We rely, again, on the wisdom of Paul:

> I appeal to you therefore, brothers and sisters, by the mercies
> of God, to present your bodies as a living sacrifice, holy
> and acceptable to God, which is your spiritual worship. Do
> not be conformed to this world, but be transformed by
> the renewing of your minds, so that you may discern what is
> the will of God—what is good and acceptable and perfect.
>
> (Romans 12:1–2)

and on the revealing beauty of our ritual prayer:

> Father, you are holy indeed,
> and all creation rightly gives you praise.
> All life, all holiness comes from you
> through your Son Jesus Christ the Lord,
> by the working of the Holy Spirit.
> From age to age you gather a people to yourself,
> so that from east to west
> a perfect offering may be made
> to the glory of your name.
> And so, Father, we bring you these gifts . . .
>
> (Eucharistic Prayer III)

The children around us would have nodded off to sleep many pages back. They have many years ahead of them to ask these questions, to hear and to tell the story. It is to be hoped, however, that the child within us has been refreshed by this exercise, as are the adults and youngsters at the Passover table. Neither our questions nor our answers are new. We have asked what has been asked for centuries and our response is as old as the questions themselves. In what may appear to be complex, let us pray that we have glimpsed what is provocatively simple.

PUTTING THEORY INTO PRACTICE

Our discussion has focused primarily on the liturgy of the eucharist celebrated by the community of the baptized. We have referred often to the "divine song of praise" Christ Jesus sings throughout all ages, the sacrifice of praise offered by the church community. That phrase is taken from the chapter in the *Constitution on the Sacred Liturgy* on the Liturgy of the Hours. We turn our attention to the Hours in order to put into practice the theory of this book's first chapter.

> The prayer of the Daily Office (Liturgy of the Hours) is part of the praise of the whole of creation offered to its Creator. Our first and ultimate vocation is to give an intelligible form to this universal praise, and the liturgy of the church, the Daily Office in particular, expresses this above all. Through the Daily Office the church unceasingly continues this expression of praise offered by the whole creation consciously or unconsciously, in spite of being enslaved to sin.[5]

Our difficulty in accepting the truth in this statement is that the prayer of the Hours has not been part of our experience; for centuries, the Liturgy of the Hours has been the preserve of religious communities and the clergy. While most of the reforms mandated by conciliar and postconciliar documents have been implemented, the mandate to restore the Hours as parish prayer has been almost universally ignored. The church's prayer is left sadly impoverished by this failure. The celebration of the Hours, with all the riches it offers us, is a shining example of what we have said about worship. We shall look at the liturgy of Evening Prayer to illustrate this.

For those who have never prayed the Hours, and for those clergy and religious accustomed to the recitation of an essentially monastic breviary,[6] following is an outline of a parish celebration of Evening Prayer.[7]

Setting

The people gather in the church and are seated in a space appropriate to their number. The seats are arranged in a circle or in rows facing each other across a center aisle, that is, in choir style; auditorium seating arrangements are inappropriate. A stand for the paschal candle is in the center; nearby is a place for a thurible or incense burner. Coals for the incense are prepared and lit before the liturgy begins. The scriptures may be enthroned.

Ministers

Someone, a pastoral figure in the community, presides at the liturgy; another serves as reader; a cantor or schola is indispensable.

The Liturgy

- When all have gathered, the paschal candle is brought in and placed in its stand.
- The presider or an assistant intones, "Light and peace in Jesus Christ our Lord," and all respond, "Thanks be to God." Other candles are lit or electric lights turned on.
- All join in singing an appropriate evening hymn.
- Cantor and people join in singing Psalm 141 with its refrain, "My prayers rise like incense, my hands like the evening offering." Incense is placed on the burning coal. The singing of the psalm is concluded with a collect prayer.
- Another suitable psalm is sung, also concluded with a collect prayer.
- Psalm 116 or another psalm of praise is sung as a doxology.

- A brief scripture passage is proclaimed; several minutes of quiet reflection follow.
- All stand to sing the Gospel canticle: Mary's song, the Magnificat. During this, the candle and the people are honored with incense.
- Intercessory prayers are sung, concluding with the Lord's prayer; the presider prays a threefold blessing upon those assembled.
- A sign of peace is exchanged.

Although there is a scripture reading, this is not a liturgy of the word. It is a service of praise and thanksgiving, an offering of prayers, song and incense. One comes to this liturgy expecting to give, not to receive. There usually is no homily. Communion is not offered. It is simply a prayer of thanksgiving at the day's end. In this liturgy we stand before our God and confess our faith in the Lord Jesus; we make an offering of incense as a sign of our prayer rising before God.

Evening Prayer and its companion, Morning Prayer, are the "hinge hours" of the daily Office, the daily prayer of the Christian community.

Mary's Song and the Prayer of Christians

In the history of our faith community, one among us truly personifies what we have said about worship. The church has always held this woman in highest esteem and presents her as a model of Christian life and prayer. When as a young virgin she was told by an angel that she would conceive by the Holy Spirit, she prayed:

> My soul magnifies the Lord, and my spirit rejoices in God my Savior,
> for he has looked with favor on the lowliness of his servant.
> Surely, from now on all generations will call me blessed;
> for the Mighty One has done great things for me, and holy is his name.

(Luke 1:47–50)

In Mary's prayer we find the basic dynamic of Christian worship: acknowledgment of God's mighty deeds on our behalf and our response of praise and thanksgiving, proclaiming God the holy One and ourselves in need of God's mercy. So deep is the Virgin's understanding of this that her own womb became the sanctuary of her encounter with the Divine. The mother of Jesus reveals in her prayer how great was her appreciation of our stance before God and of our place in the story of salvation.

The Essence of the Hours

The Christian community acknowledges the saving mystery of Jesus to be the greatest work of God's mighty arm. It is this deed in Christ which we remember, for which we give thanks and which leads us to call out and praise the name of the Holy One in creation. This is the essence of the Liturgy of the Hours. It is not something to be confined to a candle-lit space filled with clouds of incense.

> Like all liturgy, the Liturgy of the Hours is a corporate prayer, the activity of the body of the faithful. In liturgical prayer individuals join freely in making prayer together — offering personal, but not individualistic or idiosyncratic prayer. To enter into the liturgical act means forgetting one's own concerns and being present to the prayer of Christ's own body. . . . All worship is directed toward the living. The Liturgy of the Hours is no exception. Offering God time spent in "useless prayer and praise" is genuine to the extent that prayer shapes Christian living. Liturgy helps teach the Christian how to live, how to make all of life a gift offered continually and freely to God.[8]

The work of bringing the Liturgy of the Hours to its proper place as the prayer of the whole community is no small task. This is due in part to our identification of liturgy with eucharist and the other sacraments. All our sacramental worship forms all have an obvious purpose, but the Liturgy of the Hours, as Melloh suggests, is "useless" prayer and praise. It will take some time for contemporary Christians, accustomed as we are to an economy of productivity, to learn the value, depth and authenticity of such useless activity.

To celebrate the prayer of the Hours requires not only our understanding of its ritual elements, but even more our deep appreciation of what Christian worship is all about. A universal restoration of this liturgy as the prayer of local communities will signal our deepening understanding of why it is we worship whom we worship in the way that is ours as Christians.

Notes

1. Beginning with the promulgation of the *Constitution on the Sacred Liturgy* (CSL) on December 4, 1963.

2. CSL, 21. *Vatican Council II: The Basic Sixteen Documents,* revised edition. Austin Flannery OP, ed. (Northport NY: Costello Publishing Company, 1996).

3. *Environment and Art in Catholic Worship* (EACW), 29, Bishops' Committee on the Liturgy (Washington DC: United States Catholic Conference, 1978).

4. CSL, 83.

5. Les Presses de Taizé, *The Taizé Office* (Chicago: GIA Publications, Inc., 1981), 9.

6. The prayer of the Hours was originally a parochial liturgy, but only its monastic expression, through the Roman breviary, survived. CSL called for the restoration of a parochial or cathedral office as the prayer of the local church.

7. This outline is modeled on the liturgy provided in *Praise God in Song: Ecumenical Daily Prayer,* John Melloh, SM, and William Storey, eds., with musical settings by Michael Joncas, David Clark Isele and Howard Hughes, SM; (Chicago: GIA Publications, Inc., 1979).

8. John Melloh, SM, *Assembly* (Notre Dame Center for Pastoral Liturgy) 10(4): 245–246.

Chapter 2

LET'S STOP PLANNING LITURGIES!

When we speak of liturgy we speak of nothing less than the prayer of God's people: people seeking communion with the Lord as they offer their thanksgiving and praise. We are speaking of those moments when the saving mysteries of God's love for us are recounted, celebrated, shared and experienced: the communion of God's people with their Creator. The liturgy is "the summit toward which the activity of the church is directed; it is also the source from which all its power flows."[1] The liturgy is the source and summit of Christian life as it is lived and celebrated in our own communities. Nothing less than this is the business of those who make ready for and minister the sacred mysteries in our worship.

This business is a serious one and leads us to make three bold statements:

1. Liturgy cannot be planned.
2. Liturgy must always be prepared.
3. Preparing for the celebration of liturgy is a ministry and an art.

These statements need elaboration but not tempering. They mean what they say, without reservation. This chapter will explore their meaning.

Titles exert a subtle and powerful influence over the persons and tasks they denote; consider the difference between *priest* and *presbyter, Mass* and *eucharist, usher* and *minister of hospitality.* How we name ourselves and our work helps shape who we are and what we do. A critical look at a title may bring into sharp focus the way that self-perception can become self-deception.

Most of those who read these pages will have some connection with the task commonly referred to as "liturgy planning." At first glance, this seems a reasonable title: The subject of our work is the liturgy, and a good deal of that work goes on at planning meetings, with a group of people often called a planning team or committee. We presume that if there is a liturgy to be celebrated, then there is an event to be planned. Indeed, if no "planning" precedes the particular liturgy we often refer to the celebration as unplanned.

The Liturgy Is Already Planned

Before we "plan" one more liturgy, let's consider how much of our Sunday eucharist is in place before any planning team swings into action.

The Outline Every Sunday Mass begins with some form of gathering or entrance rite. This is followed by readings from scripture and a homily. The table is then prepared with bread, wine and book for the eucharistic prayer, in which all take part. All are invited to share in communion. The celebration concludes with a blessing and dismissal.

The Readings The readings are all from scripture. They are determined by the liturgical calendar and the three-year cycle of the lectionary.

Prayer Texts Texts for the eucharistic prayer, the opening prayer, the prayer over the gifts and the prayer after communion are set forth in the sacramentary.

The Dialogues All dialogue between the presiding priest and the assembly is standard and known to all present.

The Ministers A priest presides over the assembly's prayer. Designated members of the community carry out the various ministerial tasks within the celebration.

The Place In most instances, the celebration takes place in a particular and well-known place of fixed architectural dimensions. This place is furnished and decorated appropriately for liturgy.

Given all this, why do we and so many others spend countless, often difficult, hours in liturgy "planning"? Is the "planning" of liturgy a needless duplication of the work that has already been done by those who prepared the lectionary and sacramentary? Does "planning" consist only of selecting music and scheduling ministers?

This Is Good News!

It may seem, then, that planning teams have no purpose. Before we all hand in our resignations, let's look at what our investigation of a title has yielded.

- Much of our work is already done for us before the liturgy team begins its meeting.
- There is no need to duplicate what is already accomplished for us.
- We may have been making more work for ourselves than was necessary and channeling our energy in futile directions.
- Perhaps "liturgy planning" is not the best or most accurate title for the task at hand.

From these discoveries we can begin the process of reexamining our work and, perhaps, renaming ourselves. We can begin to discover how the old title has shaped our efforts in the past and how it may have caused frustration in our work.

The label "liturgy planning" is problematic if it leads us to believe that our task is to invent, devise or create the liturgy. All these paths are dead ends. Worship is not something we invent; it is the given, it is our duty, it is what we do. Prayer is not something we devise; it is a relationship. Christian ritual is not something we create; it is concerned with what we do naturally: we bathe, we eat and drink, we forgive and we marry.

We may protest that it has never been our intention, in planning the liturgy, to "invent, devise or create" it. It is at this point, however, that we need to be aware of the thin line between self-perception and self-deception: What our intention is about things and what our practice discloses are often two different realities.

An illustration may be helpful. A parish liturgy team sets about the work of planning eucharist for the Sundays of the Easter season. They have a healthy desire to let the rich celebration of the Paschal Vigil spill over into the liturgies of the coming weeks. A question arises: How do we sustain the brightness of the Paschal candle, the joy of the Gloria, and the cleansing freshness of the baptismal waters? An idea occurs: Incorporate them into the Sunday opening rites! But someone worries that the assembly will tire of the repetitious parade of these elements. A solution is proposed: On the even-numbered Sundays of Easter, the Paschal candle will be carried in procession, with the Gloria as the opening song. On the alternate Sundays, the candle will remain in its stand, near the ambo; a hymn will accompany the procession, and the Gloria will be sung during a sprinkling rite before the opening prayer!

Such an inventive device is less creative than it is manipulative—and it is the fruit of "planning." The problem here is that the team has either (a) asked the wrong questions, (b) asked no questions at all or (c) asked the right questions but with little understanding of them. The "intention" behind all this was simply "planning." The result is a hodgepodge of variations based on the assumption that the Christian assembly will quickly be bored by its own major symbols.

The Sunday Eucharist

As a title for the work we do, "liturgy planning" is simply inadequate. What, then, will more accurately describe the task of liturgy teams? Considering the Sunday eucharist may lead us in a more satisfying direction.

- Sunday eucharist is the weekly gathering of the church community for worship.
- At this service, the scriptures are proclaimed so that God's people may hear the saving and divine word as they gather at the Lord's table to be nourished and sustained for the task of going forth to continue the Lord's work.
- The eucharistic liturgy is primarily a prayer of thanksgiving to the Father, offered by the sons and daughters of the church with, through and in Christ, in the power of the Spirit.
- This prayer of thanksgiving is made in word and gesture, in song and silence, in sign and symbol, in solo voice and in chorus.
- Sunday eucharist is the church at prayer, meeting the Lord in an assembly of word, sacrament and family—a communion sealed in the covenant of the Lord's blood.

The Sunday eucharist is the ritual encounter of the church with God, who dwells in unapproachable light; it is the meeting of God's people with their Lord at a common table. This sacred meeting is not dependent on our design or plans; it is all the work of the Lord and God's Spirit moving in our midst. If grace can be defined as the quality of our relationship with God, then Sunday eucharist is surely a particularly graced moment. This graced, sacramental moment is a divine gift offered to God's people:

- Though it is we who gather for prayer, it is the Lord who calls us.

- Though it is we who read and listen for the word, it is the Lord who speaks it.
- Though it is we who offer bread and wine, these were first the Lord's gift to us.

None of us is able to cry out, "Abba, Father," unless the Spirit first moves us to do so. God's Spirit moves where it wills, when it wills, how it wills. Although we are unable to plan our encounter with the Lord, we are called, always and every-where, to be ready, open to, and prepared to encounter the Lord who comes to meet us — and this is our duty and our salvation.

Although we are unable to plan the graced moment of encounter with the Lord, we are obliged to prepare for it. Each person, and the whole community, is called to "prepare the way of the Lord" and to make straight the paths along which we encounter the divine Traveler.

This brings us to a new title for the work of liturgy teams. Let's stop "planning liturgies" and let's begin to prepare for worship.

LITURGY MUST ALWAYS BE PREPARED

To celebrate the liturgy without preparation is a violation of God's holy presence and a crime against those who gather to celebrate that presence. That may seem harsh, but the words have been chosen carefully and deliberately, with the hope that we will begin to see that the difference between the words "planning" and "preparing" is neither capricious nor is it marginal; it is much more than a question of semantics.

To say that unprepared liturgy is a violation of God's holy presence is to acknowledge that the liturgical act is awesome indeed. In the liturgy, we discover ourselves in the presence of the Most High God. We find ourselves on holy ground but, unlike Moses, we tread that ground with our feet shod and we come face to face with the living God. We speak freely that name which the high priest in Israel spoke but once a year; we name the Lord whose own we have been named. We look into

the eyes of the Lord and we do not die—we live! This may
be an unfamiliar way of expressing what we do in liturgy. The
color of these remarks is unabashedly Byzantine; we in the
Latin rite might do well to study the spirit in which our brothers
and sisters in the Eastern rites offer their worship.

A Sacred Trust

Unprepared celebration of the liturgy is a crime against those
who gather to celebrate God's holy presence. In the Christian
scheme of things, members of the community depend and
rely on one another to minister to the community's needs. Those
who assume positions of service in the community are given a
sacred trust by those whom they serve.

Those who prepare and minister the liturgy are entrusted
with the moments when the church will enter and tread on that
holy ground which is the Lord's. Because that holy ground is
the Lord's, the task of preparing worship is a sacred one. To
approach that task with less than awe is to trivialize the ministry and to violate the community's trust. This is nothing less
than a crime in the highest of all courts. The work at stake
here is intimately bound up with our duty and our salvation.
Liturgy teams and ministers are charged with preparing a
time, a place and a table for the graced encounter of God and
God's people. It is the task, the ministry, of the liturgy team to:

- prepare a place where the community gathers for worship; to
  ready that holy ground, that house of God's people where
  Creator and created meet.
- prepare for the proclamation of the scriptures so that the
  gathered assembly may hear the Lord's saving word.
- prepare the music of praise and prayer so that all may join in
  singing the divine canticle of the One who saves us.
- prepare the table and the table prayer so that all may join in
  offering thanks to the Lord who sups with sinners.
- prepare bread and wine, a simple meal, so that all might be
  nourished by the bread of angels and the cup of salvation.

• prepare a moment that invites the community to praise and helps to prepare believers for communion with the Lord and one another.

Liturgy cannot be planned. It must always be prepared, made ready. While "planning liturgy" may be a misguided and frustrating experience, it is a relatively easy task when compared with the alternative of preparing for worship. This ministry of preparing is no simple task; it is a craft, and this brings us to our third area of concern.

PREPARING FOR LITURGY IS A MINISTRY AND AN ART

The ministry of preparing for worship calls for time, energy, patience, understanding and much prayer; it demands, at times, creativity and ingenuity. In all this, the work must be discreetly ordered toward the service of God and God's people at prayer. The discretion required here is the kind that goes into the preparation for a dinner party where the guests easily enjoy one another and the meal; where all the details, large and small alike, contribute to the whole event; where the graciousness of the evening covers any breach of etiquette; where the host is responsible for everything and yet appears to be concerned only with enjoying the repast with gathered friends. This is an art![2]

The ministry of preparing for worship is a comparable art:

• It is modest, as modest as the art of living with, and not above, one's neighbor.
• It is basic, as basic as the art of knowing when to serve and when to allow oneself to be served.
• It is skilled, as skilled as sitting at table and managing to engage in conversation with some flair while at the same time ingesting food through the mouth.
• It is indispensable, as indispensable as the art of learning and living with the graceful manners that support, enhance, and strengthen the social bonds of life.

The materials involved in this art of preparing for worship are simple and profound: faith in God; an appreciation for things whole, true and beautiful; love of neighbor; and love for that heritage of prayer which is ours as Christians. Like all good art, this liturgical art is not self-interested and is never self-indulgent. It is ever an act of love, a service done for the glory of God and the good of others. Like fine art, this liturgical artistry is useless; it has no orientation toward productivity. It neither seeks nor accepts compensation of any kind, for the doing of the art is its own reward.

The Discipline of Beauty

Such artistry is neither abstract nor obscure. It is practiced in real communities of real people who fashion false idols and often forget their manners. This artistry struggles to flourish in such surroundings. We fail often as we practice our artistry, for we are more practiced in the art of pleasing ourselves than we are practiced in the discipline of true beauty.

The discipline of things beautiful is not something that comes naturally to us; that naturalness fell apart when we prized the apple of power and knowledge over the rest of Eden's fruit. Instead, we need to rehearse the right and mannered order of things: We need to gather often, in a posture of praise, in the Creator's holy presence. We need to learn to dance upon that holy ground with measured and graceful step, and to speak the name of the Holy One with hushed reverence and joyful shouts. And we need to do all this through, with and in Christ, the first fruit of that new and redeemed creation.

While the title "preparing for worship" may focus more clearly on the work that is ours and channel more effectively the time and energy we invest, it also challenges us to a deeper level of involvement. "Preparing for liturgy" is not merely a skill to be learned; it is an art whose subtle craft is intuited, discovered and matured in the context of the church's life and prayer. Knowledge of, and an appreciation for, the tradition of that prayer's history is the indispensable honing of this craft. This is the tradition that the contemporary community maintains with fidelity, celebrates with freshness and hands on to the next generation with hope. Worship and its preparation flourish in the hands of artists and die in the hands of practitioners.

PATRON SAINTS FOR THOSE WHO PREPARE FOR WORSHIP

There is no scriptural basis for the "liturgy planning team." Luke's gospel, however, offers us Peter and John as models or patrons for those whose ministry it is to prepare for liturgy.

> Then came the day of Unleavened Bread, on which the Passover lamb had to be sacrificed. So Jesus sent Peter and John, saying, "Go and *prepare* the Passover meal for us that we may eat it." They asked him, "Where do you want us to *make preparations* for it?" "Listen," he said to them, "when you have entered the city, a man carrying a jar of water will meet you; follow him into the house he enters, and say to the owner of the house, 'The teacher asks you, "Where is the guest room, where I may eat the Passover with my disciples?"' He will show you a large room upstairs, already furnished. *Make preparations* for us there." So they went and found everything as he told them; and they *prepared* the Passover meal.
>
> (Luke 22:7–13, emphasis added)

Peter and John certainly had no inkling of what would happen at that supper table, and much less might they have planned what was about to happen. The two simply prepared the room and the food. It was the Lord who gave himself to his friends in bread broken and cup poured out. Peter and John ministered, and their service, like art, was modest, basic, skilled and indispensable. Their work was simple and profound. Their service was neither self-interested nor self-indulgent: They acted upon the Lord's request for the good of the other disciples. What they did — prepare a place — was no elaborate production. They had no delusions of grandeur as they swept the room and set the table—routine, menial tasks. The art of doing what the Lord had asked was its own reward.

The artistry of Peter and John is our ministry; the gift of Jesus at that table in an upper room is our inheritance.

Saint Peter, Saint John, pray for us!

Notes

1. *Constitution on the Sacred Liturgy*, 10.
2. I am indebted here to Aidan Kavanagh's wisdom in his address to the Annual Conference of the Notre Dame Center for Pastoral Liturgy in 1977.

Chapter 3

SPEAKING *of* LITURGY

I used to minister in a parish where 90 percent of the members were college students. This prompted many people outside the parish to ask if the students were coming to Sunday Mass. Upon hearing that our church was nearly full three times each Sunday, those inquiring often responded, "That's wonderful! Your liturgies must be informal and contemporary." The students themselves often commented that our services were more "meaningful" than the "formal and traditional" Masses they experienced at home. Those responsible for preparing our Sunday eucharists were puzzled by such comments because our celebrations were grounded in the same liturgical books, the lectionary and sacramentary, used by parishes everywhere.

When speaking of liturgy, we find ourselves and others using many adjectives — traditional, contemporary, formal, informal, creative — to describe various experiences. Giving some definition to these widely used terms should lead to a better understanding of worship in general and the worship we experience in particular.

LABELS OLD AND NEW

In the days before the liturgical reforms of the Second Vatican Council, particular celebrations of the eucharist were classified as low, high and solemn high Masses. Since then, new, if unofficial, tags have attached themselves to our celebrations — formal and informal, traditional and contemporary. While such labels mean different things to the different people who apply them, there is a commonly accepted understanding of these terms in American parish life.

We saw earlier how powerfully titles shape how we understand who we are and what we do. For the same reasons, we need to be wary of their influence on our liturgy. Labels can be good and helpful if they rise out of the nature of worship, but categories imposed from outside misdirect the worship we offer. The liturgy has its own focus: the paschal mystery of Jesus' dying and rising. Imposing labels or themes that try to force the liturgy to focus elsewhere or mean something else misdirect us.

How, then, are we to understand the categories of traditional and contemporary, formal and informal?[1] Do they rise out of the liturgy itself, or are they imposed from the outside? These questions are not merely academic. The potential problems reach critical proportions when criteria from outside our worship begin to shape the liturgical act and the worshiping community. This happens more often than we may realize, and the instances may tell us more about our worship than we care to know. We are all familiar with parish communities that are divided into camps according to such labels; a house divided against itself, especially a house of prayer, can neither stand nor long endure.

LITURGY AND TIME

In the first chapter I told the story of a wedding anniversary celebration, illustrating the saying, "Remembering is a form of meeting." Remembering *(anamnesis)* is at the core of Christian worship, and it can teach us something of the Christian notion of time. The "worship moment" is always a confluence of the past, the present and the future. This lyric says it well:

> We remember how you loved us to your death
> and still we celebrate for you are with us here,

and we believe that we will see you when you come
in your glory, Lord: we remember, we celebrate, we believe.[2]

We remember what the Lord has done for us (the past); we
proclaim the Lord who saves us (the present); we look forward
to the fulfillment of the reign of God (the future). When we
gather at the Lord's table to celebrate the meal of the new covenant, "we do this in memory of Jesus Christ, our passover and
our lasting peace."[3] We remember and we do what he did
on the night he was betrayed. All of this is celebrated at the
table that is a sign for us of that table in heaven where the communion feast of the reconciled will have no end.

To celebrate the eucharist, then, is to carry on the tradition that flowed forth from the wounds of the Crucified, that
was prefigured at supper on the night before his death, and
that lives yet in the sacrifice of praise that we offer. What we do
at eucharist is as traditional as the Paschal mystery itself and
as contemporary as the Lord who is present in the breaking of
the bread and the blessing of the cup.

Traditional Liturgy

To speak of Christian liturgy as "traditional" is to border on
the redundant. Our word *tradition* has its roots in the Latin
verb *tradere:* to give up, to transmit, to hand on. The divine service we offer is precisely this kind of activity. Paul speaks elo-
quently to the Corinthians in these words:

> I received from the Lord what I also handed on to you, that
> the Lord Jesus on the night when he was betrayed took a loaf
> of bread, and when he had given thanks, he broke it and
> said, "This is my body that is for you. Do this in remembrance
> of me." In the same way he took the cup also, after supper,
> saying, "This cup is the new covenant in my blood. Do this,
> as often as you drink it, in remembrance of me." For as often
> as you eat this bread and drink the cup, you proclaim the
> Lord's death until he comes.
>
> (1 Corinthians 11:23–26)

Paul is articulate about his "handing on" of the tradition of the Lord's supper. Each time we celebrate the eucharist we do the same kind of "handing on," although with greater subtlety. In the eucharist we continue to "proclaim the Lord's death until he comes." Our liturgy itself is this proclamation, and it is this, along with the preaching of the gospel and the work of justice, that hands on from generation to generation the good news of Jesus Christ, the glad tidings of salvation.

To celebrate the eucharist, especially as the culmination of baptismal initiation, is about as traditional as any Christian community can be. At the tables of word and sacrament we rehearse that ancient story of God's love for creation and of God's mercy on those who would pervert what has been given us. What we do in the Sunday assembly is as old as the faith itself. In nearly 2,000 years the form of what we do has known many changes, but three elements have survived all our whims and fancies: the telling of the story, our prayer of thanksgiving and the sharing of the meal.

Contemporary Liturgy

To say that liturgy is "contemporary" means more than that it is celebrated in the present day (*com* + *temporarius*: with the time). Liturgy is contemporary inasmuch as it reveals and makes present in our own time the saving mystery of Jesus and offers life to those who would repent and believe the good news. That the liturgy is contemporary is not something that depends upon those who celebrate it; divine service is contemporary precisely because it is the ministry of the risen Christ who sings his canticle of divine praise throughout all ages. As the presider prays while inscribing the Paschal candle at the Easter Vigil:

> Christ yesterday and today,
> the beginning and the end,
> Alpha and Omega.
> All time belongs to him
> and all the ages.

To him be glory and power
through every age for ever.
Amen.

We say that liturgy is contemporary because through it:

- God continues to gather a people from east to west so that a perfect offering may be made to the glory of that most holy Name.
- The voice and word of the Lord continue to be addressed to all peoples in all times.
- The reconciling ministry of Jesus crucified pours out its healing upon those whose lives and hearts are breaking.
- The work of justice, accomplished in the mystery of Jesus' dying and rising, is proclaimed as comfort and hope for today's oppressed.
- The Lord and sinners are together at the table today, as when the Son of Mary supped with tax collectors and prostitutes.

Our divine service is contemporary because it is the prayer of the One who was in the beginning, is now and evermore will be—in the power of the Spirit of all that is Holy.

Traditional and Contemporary

We have tried to define "traditional and contemporary" in a way that is faithful to the liturgy they describe. Here, as throughout these pages, we are making the effort to return to the basics, to learn again the root meaning of the worship we offer and to understand its place in the life of the Christian community. In light of what we have said thus far, we offer the modest thesis that worship in each community must be both traditional and contemporary.

It is the Lord, through the power of the Spirit, who makes of our worship contemporary liturgy. Thus, a parish community at prayer (and those who prepare for and minister in that prayer) must celebrate a contemporary liturgy. The Lord will not be held back from gathering, speaking to, reconciling and justifying those who assemble to offer divine service, either in spite of, or with the help of, our preparation and ministry.

Of course, there is much that we can do to assist the spiritual exchange between God and God's people at prayer; to do any less is a crime against God's people and a violation of that holy ground upon which they tread. The Lord will come with our help or without it, but it is the task of ministers to ready the people for the Lord's holy advent. In the gospel parable, all ten bridal attendants were present when the groom arrived; only five had oil for their lamps and . . . well, we know the rest of the story.

In a like way, our worship is always a traditional liturgy, in that it tells the story and gathers us to prayer and the Lord's supper. Traditional liturgy hands on the life of faith through *anamnesis* and proclamation. When, however, the *anamnesis* is so hidden or boring that it becomes amnesia, or when the proclamation of the Lord's death is little more than a muted whisper, then "criminal charges" may justly be brought against those responsible for such a travesty. Traditional liturgy hands on its life when the gospel is preached boldly and when ritual is celebrated with such strength that all can see for themselves the mystery of Jesus dying and rising, breaking and pouring out himself in the life of the community and upon the table around which the community gathers.

The community that celebrates this kind of traditional and contemporary liturgy will soon find:

- that it is less concerned about what instrument accompanies the opening song and more concerned about gathering the lost into the fold that celebrates the opening rite.
- that it is less concerned whether the song during the preparation of the gifts is a Latin motet or a Shaker hymn and more concerned about what percentage of parish resources is allocated for the poor.
- that it is less concerned about how high the gospel book is carried in the procession and more concerned about how the Lord's word is calling for healing of the community's wounds.

This is admittedly a tall order and a great hope, but the divine service we offer calls us to nothing less. All this and more is possible in the company of the Lord, through, with and in whom all our prayer and work is offered and accomplished.

THE POPULAR SENSE OF "TRADITIONAL" AND "CONTEMPORARY"

Having seen how the terms "traditional" and "contemporary" best address the worship question, we look now to the popular sense in which these terms are used to describe worship experience and style. Certain polarities will surface in the discussion as a case is made for a confluence of styles and for unity in the assembly's prayer.

Because of the broad range of experiences in American worship, and because these two terms are understood subjectively, simple definitions on this popular level are impossible. The two lists that follow are designed to help the reader situate his or her community's liturgical program in a context for discussion.

"Traditional" Liturgy

American communities and ministers who believe the worship they celebrate to be "traditional" probably fall into one or more of the following groups.

1. communities and ministers who believe that something valuable was lost in the reforms of Vatican II
2. communities and ministers who find value in celebrating the liturgy strictly as the liturgical books direct
3. communities and ministers who believe that our worship forms must be preserved and that the preservation of these forms is easily threatened by variation from the norm
4. communities and ministers who believe that almost everything was lost in the reforms of Vatican II
5. communities and ministers who believe that what some call the growth of an "American liturgical experience" is little more than a passing fad, a stage we are going through

6. communities and ministers who believe that fidelity (defined as strict adherence in every detail) in all matters liturgical is a sign of fidelity to the church, its mission and its hierarchy
7. communities and ministers who celebrate according to the revised rites but in a minimalist fashion

"Contemporary" Liturgy

American communities who understand the worship they celebrate to be "contemporary" probably fall into one or more of the following groups.

1. communities and ministers who believe that the reforms of Vatican II made a valuable contribution to the life of the church and its worship
2. communities and ministers who find value in celebrating the liturgy with the needs of the local church in mind
3. communities and ministers who believe that the options provided in the rites (and some of local invention) help worship life to thrive and grow
4. communities and ministers who believe that no "real" liturgy existed between the Edict of Constantine and Vatican II
5. communities and ministers who evaluate their worship in terms of what is suggested at the most recent workshop or convention
6. communities and ministers who believe that fidelity to the church's shared mission of peace and justice is of utmost concern
7. communities and ministers who reject any liturgical prayer, style or musical composition of preconciliar origin

With the exception of numbers 4, 5 and 7 in both lists, I suggest that the communities and ministers in all the other groups have a valuable contribution to make to our discussion. There are, in these groups, varying degrees of appreciation and knowledge of the history of worship in our faith tradition. Some err on the side of caution, others on the side of spiritual adventure. There are also several approaches to the church's mission and to the relationship of the local community to the church universal.

Neither of the two preceding lists is perfect or complete; they each betray certain prejudices. Some will easily raise objections to what has been described as traditional or contemporary. But before the quick and defensive criticism rises to the lips, let us call to mind our sins and prepare to offer one another a sign of the Lord's peace and mercy. We (all of us) form the family of those who confess one Lord, one faith and one baptism, one God who is creator of us all. Can we not make the effort to see what our brothers and sisters have to teach us before we raise a critical brow? Is it not past the time when we need to scrutinize one another's liturgical expression? How long will we be so proud as to presume that those who don't do it "our way" are hopelessly behind the times, liturgical simpletons who have not yet seen the light (our light)? When we move to a new community or travel on vacation, how long will we continue to pursue that futile quest for a parish that celebrates "like at home"? When will we learn to be gracious hosts and courteous guests?

> Now in the following instructions I do not commend you, because when you come together it is not for the better but for the worse. For, to begin with, when you come together as a church, I hear that there are divisions among you, and to some extent I believe it. . . . When you come together, it is not really to eat the Lord's supper. For when the time comes to eat, each of you goes ahead with your own supper. . . . What should I say to you? Should I commend you? In this matter I do not commend you!
>
> (1 Corinthians 11:17–18, 20–21, 22e)

Indeed, there are divisions among us, and many are centered on how we celebrate the Lord's Supper. What Paul would write today to the church in the United States might well be a letter we would rather not open. We are at pains here not to nominate either traditional or contemporary liturgy for an award in "Best Style in Worship—1990s." Rather, we are urging that the best of each style be brought together to create one great river of worship flowing through the broad landscape of American worship. We need to learn from one another.

In some communities, the whole of the liturgical schedule might be described as either "traditional" or "contemporary." In others some celebrations are prepared to be "traditional," and others to be "contemporary." Neither plan is healthy or pastoral. There is the danger in both cases that the stylistic consideration, "traditional" or "contemporary," becomes the one criterion in preparing for and celebrating the liturgy. It is a sad thought that an element that could lead the community to prayer and worship might be precluded on the grounds of an arbitrary stylistic judgment.

Leave All Things You Have

A personal anecdote makes this case with poignancy. Some time ago, a friend came to my office and asked me to suggest a song that his folk ensemble might include in a liturgy celebrating the vows of several women religious. I asked if he knew Suzanne Toolan's delightful composition, "How Brightly Deep!" with its lilting refrain, "Leave all things you have and come and follow me!"[4] Unfamiliar with the piece, he asked if I had a copy of it on hand. I reached for the large red hymnal on my bookshelf and he said, "Oh, well, we don't really do that kind of music." Having heard only one line of the song's lyric and none of its melody, he was ready to reject the piece because of the book in which it was printed! We, all of us, have much to leave behind as we ready ourselves to join in the song which the Lord sings in the halls of heaven.

FORMAL AND INFORMAL

As soon as one speaks of formal or informal worship, images of each are quickly drawn in the mind's eye. Before we deal with this popular imagery, however, a look at some definitions will help get us to the root of the issues at hand in this study.

forma (Latin): mold, shape, beauty

form, *n.* 1. the shape or outline of anything; figure; structure, excluding color, texture and density . . . 4. the particular way of being that gives something its nature or character; combination of qualities making something what it is; intrinsic character . . . 7. an established or customary way of acting or behaving; ceremony; ritual . . .

formal, *adj.* 1. of external form or structure, rather than nature or content; apparent. 2. of the internal form; relating to the character or nature; essential. 3. of or according to prescribed or fixed customs, rules, ceremonies . . . 7. very regular or orderly in arrangements, pattern, etc., rigidly symmetrical . . .

informal, *adj.* 1. not formal, specifically, a) not according to prescribed or fixed customs rules, ceremonies, etc. b) casual, easy, unceremonious, or relaxed. c) designed for use or wear on everyday occasions; colloquial[5]

Consider the number of bells that these phrases ring in our liturgical context. Then consider that these definitions come not from a theological glossary but from *Webster's New World Dictionary*.

Of particular interest are the definitions that appear to be in conflict with one another. "Form" can refer to either the external or internal qualities of what is being described. The primary reference, for our purpose, is to the internal. When speaking of the formal nature of liturgy, we need to ask what it is that relates to the "essential character" of worship that gives the liturgical act its shape, outline, order and structure. This is not to argue that worship should be formal but simply to acknowledge that there is a form in worship which must be understood before a case is made for formal or informal worship.

Christ at the Center

The form of Christian worship is, simply, the Paschal mystery of Jesus' dying and rising. Jesus is the "essential character and nature" of the worship we offer — our worship is offered through, with and in him. All discussion of formal and informal worship must begin with this acknowledgment of the Christic nature or form of liturgical prayer and action. Even the assembly of believers that offers the worship is itself the body of Christ. In this most basic sense, then, all worship is formal insofar as Christ is its essential character.

Conversely, that which is not according to the form — that is, worship that is not essentially characterized in the person and mystery of Jesus — is simply not worship. In this sense, and at this basic level, informal liturgy is outside the boundary of Christian worship.

Keep in mind, here, that we are not speaking of *formal* and *informal* in the popular sense. We are trying, again, to get back to the basics of worship. All too often our time and energy (and squabbles!) are invested on the secondary level with no reference to, and sometimes at the expense of, the more important issue. Moving to a more fundamental level may help us better understand worship in general and its attendant popular images in particular.

FORMALITY AND INFORMALITY

One way to distinguish between the primary and secondary levels is to speak of the primary, internal form as *formal* and *informal,* and of the secondary, external form in terms of *formality* and *informality.* Here the popular images are the stuff of the discussion, but not without further reference to Christ as the true form of worship.

Using the dictionary definitions again, we might understand formality in worship to be ritual prayer celebrated in an established and customary fashion. By the same token, informality in worship might be described as ritual prayer that tends to depart from prescribed or fixed customs and rules. Our own postconciliar worship and its supporting documentation seems to encourage us in both directions. Certainly there are prescribed ways of celebrating the liturgy, but ample room is given, within some bounds, for variation and degrees of solemnity and choice.

What the contemporary literature warns against is also found in the dictionary offerings: rigidity and unceremonious colloquialism. When formality and informality become the molds for shaping our liturgical prayer then the potential for the extremes of rigidity and casualness are great — precisely because formality and informality override the inherent Christic form, which makes worship what it is. What is at stake here is the meshing of the human and divine that is so perfectly accomplished in Christ and so easily and often ill-proportioned in ourselves.

Mechanical and Trivial

Formality in worship may run the risk of becoming mechanical and less than human, and thus unchristian. Undue attention to detail in ceremony or the canonization of a particular musical genre, for example, may take place at the expense of the prayer that ritual and music are intended to serve, not dominate. Informality in worship runs a similar risk when laxity in details threatens to trivialize the divine service to be offered. Canonization of a musical genre is a temptation and danger at this end of the spectrum, too. While formality in worship may be uninviting to some, informality based on a personal "style" may render the service inaccessible to all but an inner circle of devotees.

Danger in the extremes is obvious, but what of the middle ground? Is there not an elasticity within our worship that allows for a healthy tension between formality and informality? There is indeed, and this brings us to the question of styles of worship.

STYLES OF WORSHIP

In every city and resort town across the country, parishes receive phone calls from visitors each weekend asking for the Mass schedule. Some inquire further: "What kind of Mass do you have at 10:00?" "Holy" and "Roman Catholic" are not the answers they are looking for. There is, of course, some cause for rejoicing in the knowledge that people care about the manner in which the eucharist is celebrated. Still, we should be wary when people choose their community and place of worship based on style.

Styles of worship abound, and they accommodate the temperament, personality, culture and faith experience of particular communities. This is as it should be. It is the community's personality and life that enter the holy place to offer worship. Indeed, true worship cannot be validly offered except out of the stuff of our life together. All that is human bears the hallmark of styles. The most powerful experience of the sacred is to be found in the action of the assembly; therefore, we should expect that worship will reflect that community's style. Nevertheless, when the community's personality (and its style of expression) becomes a preeminent consideration in our worship, we risk slipping into spiritual amnesia, forgetting who we worship, how we worship and why we worship in the first place.

Style and Authenticity

You will find here no argument for a uniform and universal style of worship; that worship would be inauthentic. Worship styles are such important considerations precisely because they are tools for judging the truth and validity of our divine service. It must be remembered, however, that a community's style of worship is not something that the liturgy committee members discover at a diocesan workshop; it is a living reality that rises up out of the prayer, work and experience of the local believing community as it is shaped by its heritage and its union with the larger church. In this way, the local community's style of worship is authenticated by the genuineness with which that style is expressive of the people's faith experience and by its fidelity to the history and current liturgical practice of its sister communities in the faith.

The most important consideration of worship style, then, is authenticity. Each community must develop its own style of worship, which becomes its own formality: It is a form representative of who that community is and what it brings to prayer out of its shared life and work. At the same time, this formality in worship appropriate to the community must never become idiosyncratic; it must always allow enough informality that the visiting brother and sister can be at home with the community's prayer. The balance between formality and informality is achieved when the community develops its style with serious attention and reverence for that form of worship that is our heritage in the rites of our tradition. In this way, the worship of the local church is ever in harmony with the church at large, and the tables of word and sacrament are recognizable wherever we may travel.

Style and Honesty

Each community is obliged to worship in a way that is an honest reflection of its life and experience in the wake of the gospel's call and in its carrying out the gospel mission. All this is rooted deeply in the Paschal mystery. Thus the reflection of the community, which the liturgy is, is not only of the present moment; it also reveres the past and hopes for the future. Thus, the song of the worshiping community might well include old and even ancient hymns. Such hymns are maintained in the community's repertoire not for the sake of nostalgia, however, but precisely because they continue to be valid and valuable expressions of community prayer. If such hymns fail to satisfy this important requirement, they must be dropped. In the same way, hymnody of all generations must consistently draw us to that vision of life eternal that is ours as we gather at the Lord's table. Lyrics that celebrate only the present moment are already passé in the Christian scheme of things.

Importing worship elements from another age or culture, or from a piety or theology that our church has outgrown or developed to greater maturity, is a temptation from which we should pray to be delivered. We must come to community prayer dressed in clothes well-worn by our life's work. We worship best when the lyrics of our song are scriptural or speak poetically in the idiom of our life together in Christ. Our thanksgiving must be in the language of our hearts and lives so that we may grow to cherish the prayer we offer. Literally and figuratively, the bread that we break should be bread that we have baked.

Style and Division

Note that we have been addressing the overall style of worship within a given community. Authenticity in worship style is poorly served in a community that schedules, for instance, a "contemporary" Mass at 10:00 and a "traditional" Mass at 11:30. Schedules of this kind are often intended to serve different groups of people in the parish.

Consider, however, the division in the community where one Sunday assembly worships in a "traditional" fashion and another in a "contemporary" style — by design and intent. If we cannot learn to sing one another's songs and if we cannot learn to join in one another's prayer, how do we expect to share in the Lord's healing and reconciling ministry?

Reminding ourselves that the ideal situation would be one celebration of the eucharist on the Lord's day for which the entire community would assemble, we can envision that a single Sunday eucharist would call for a confluence of styles, yielding a wonderfully woven tapestry of the community's prayer. Granted, a confluence of styles requires much work, time and sacrifice, but anything less than this borders dangerously on remaining self-serving, self-gratifying and self-centered — all of which is alien to the heart of Christian worship.

Style and Unity

Many parishes work toward this confluence of styles once a year for the liturgies of Holy Week. This is, of course, very much as it should be, particularly on those days when only one solemn liturgy is to be celebrated in each community. At the Easter Vigil, all voices, prayers and styles make the effort to be one, each group offering its gifts and its varied talents, its prayer and its artistry. Unfortunately, the second Sunday of Easter usually finds this harmonious community once again divided according to taste, style and preference. If the Sunday assembly is the weekly remembrance of that greatest and most solemn of all feasts, that "holy night [that] dispels all evil, washes guilt away and restores lost innocence,"[6] then how can we justify, under the new rubrics of style and preference, the dividing of the community that celebrated that Vigil of all vigils with one heart, one voice and one prayer?

This is a hard saying. The intent is to prompt an honest, hard look at the different ways in which an individual community celebrates the eucharist on a given Sunday. Are we working toward a unity in parish prayer? If not, what is the balance between authentic diversity and divisive exclusivity? The following list of questions may help in coming to terms with the issues involved.

- A variety of worship styles exists in American parishes and in those around the world—styles that justifiably claim fidelity to the liturgical books. What are these styles? How are they justified? What has been our style (styles)? How do we justify them?
- Liturgy is the celebration of the Christ event, which is the ultimate work of justice in creation. What connections are there and should there be between our worship and our community's share in the work of justice?
- In what ways might our community's worship be more truly traditional and contemporary? How might our worship be more faithful to the form of liturgical prayer (the Paschal mystery of Jesus)?
- How can we work toward celebrating Sunday eucharist in our parish as one people, praying and singing with one voice?
- What do we need to bring into our worship? Of what do we need to let go? Are we willing to pray for the gift to know the difference and to do what we must to offer a fitting sacrifice of praise?

These are difficult questions, not to be taken lightly or answered quickly. Our response, in theory and practice, may be several years in coming. We did not get this far in the twinkling of an eye! The result, however, will be well worth the work, effort and time. To engage ourselves and our communities in this process will not be easy; it will require of us that which is at the heart of the liturgy — sacrifice. In all of this we need always to remember that ours is a sacred trust and we tread on holy ground.

CREATIVE LITURGY

No discussion of worship, whether formal or informal, traditional or contemporary, will go very far before the notion of "creative liturgy" makes its way into the conversation. Most often, the word *creative* makes its appearance with *informal* or *contemporary*. Seldom do we hear a service described as "formal and creative," although on occasion one might speak of a liturgical experience that was "formal, *but* creative." There is a presumption at work here that deserves our notice: That "creative" liturgy must be celebrated in an informal style precisely because it is presumed that "creative" worship somehow violates (if only benignly) the given "form" of a particular celebration. The corollary is that worship "by the book" does not admit of creativity.

Because the word *creative* enjoys an etymological kinship with the words *creator* and *creation,* it might be worth our while to investigate its meaning.

When speaking of "creative liturgy," we often mean some form of worship marked by the unusual or by some novelty. While dictionary definitions would support this use of the word *creative,* we look, for our purposes, to the primary definitions: "having the power or quality of creating; productive of."[7] This brings us within striking distance of a simple thesis: All liturgy is, of its nature, creative.

All liturgy has the power of creating; therefore, all liturgy is creative liturgy. The tautology is intentional. We need to tune our ears to appreciate this understanding and to disabuse ourselves of the notion that "creative" has principally to do with novelty or departure from the norm. To get at the root of creative liturgy we turn our attention to that member of the Trinity who has been given short shrift thus far in these pages, the Spirit of all that is Holy.

> Let your Spirit come upon these gifts to make them holy . . .
> And so Father, we bring you these gifts. We ask you to make them holy by the power of your Spirit . . .
>
> Grant that we, who are nourished by his body and blood may be filled with his Holy Spirit and become one body, one spirit in Christ.
>
> Father, may this Holy Spirit sanctify these offerings.
>
> Lord . . . by your Holy Spirit gather all who share this bread and wine into the one body of Christ, a living sacrifice of praise.[8]

Because it is our duty and our salvation, we offer praise and thanksgiving to the Father through, with and in Christ, in the power of the Holy Spirit. What would be our prayer apart from the gift of God's Spirit? None of us cries out, "Abba, Father!" unless first the Spirit moves us to do so (Romans 8:15). Every lifting of the heart, mind and soul to God is prompted by the Spirit; even the plea we make for help when we cannot pray is made at the urging of the Spirit. This urging is ever upon us, never ceasing, probing always even the hardest and coldest of hearts. The Spirit moves when it wills, where it wills and how it wills: always and everywhere.

While each of us has known the subtle and not-so-subtle ways in which the Spirit moves in our own lives, it may be difficult for us to see how this same Spirit moves the community to prayer. The work of the Spirit is often a surprise; it comes when we least expect it and in unexpected ways. The community's prayer is seldom a surprise to us: It is a scheduled event, announced in the parish bulletin. We come to this prayer for reasons that vary in their degrees of sincerity and sanctity: church law, custom and tradition, peer or family pressure, ministerial schedules, the desire to worship.

I do not want to preclude or presume the Spirit's guidance in the work of those who plan the schedule of parish prayer, nor do I suggest that the Spirit works overtime on Sunday mornings, rousing sleepy Christians from their well-deserved slumber and whispering in their ears, "It's time to praise your God!" What I do suggest is that the Spirit moves mightily in the heart of the assembly gathered for the eucharist on the Lord's day.

Gift and Pledge

If you love me, you will keep my commandments. And I will ask the Father, and he will give you another Advocate to be with you forever. This is the Spirit of truth, whom the world cannot receive, because it neither sees him nor knows him. You know him because he abides with you and he will be in you.

(John 14:15–17)

At a table in an upper room, moments before his betrayal, Jesus promises to the church the Spirit of truth, who we will recognize within us. The pledge of the gift of the Spirit has been faithfully kept; what remains to be seen is our ability to recognize this gift in our midst.

While the gathering of the Sunday assembly may be attributed to custom, schedule or the Spirit, only the Spirit can be held accountable for the prayer that is offered once the parish is assembled. No assembly cries out, "Abba, Father!" unless first the Spirit moves it to do so. Only the power of the Spirit is strong enough to encourage and enable us to tread that holy ground where Creator encounters creation. Only the Spirit of truth empowers us to assume that stance that is ours before God, the stance of the empty-handed who come to offer thanks and to pay the debt that is paid already by the One to whom we owe so much.

- It is the Spirit who helps us see that in the opening rite we gather not like the crowd at the bus stop or the local theater, but as the people of God.
- It is the Spirit who opens the ears of our hearts and minds so that in the liturgy of the word we hear more than "readings"; we hear the voice of God who speaks a saving and mercy-filled word.
- It is the Spirit of the risen Christ who does the work of uniting us in the eucharistic prayer, in that canticle of divine praise that Jesus sings forever in the halls of heaven.
- It is the Spirit of our crucified and risen brother who helps us recognize in the breaking of bread and in the blessing of a cup, the body and blood of the One broken and poured out for us so that we might have life and have it to the full.
- It is the Spirit of God who helps us believe that "we, though many throughout the world, are one body in this one Lord."[9]
- It is the Spirit who sends us from this holy table to live and work in that world which does not accept (because it does not recognize) the Spirit of truth who commissions us.

Without the power of the Spirit, our Sunday assembly would be merely an empty exercise in ritualistic, ceremonial behavior—which is just what it may appear to be to those who do not recognize the Paraclete. The question for ourselves is this: Have we who recognize the gift of the Spirit in our individual lives come to recognize the gift of this same Spirit in our communal life? This is another instance where we have much to learn from our brothers and sisters in the eastern churches. We might take a few cues, too, from those in the charismatic renewal, who so joyfully revel in the Spirit's gifts.

The Holy Spirit is the life-force in our liturgical prayer; understanding and appreciating this role is of paramount importance to those who offer divine service. Our worship is the work of the promised Paraclete among us and within us. As worshiping families, we are in dire need of catechesis on this point. As those who prepare for and minister in the liturgical

act, we need to develop a working knowledge of and relationship with this divine Ally who comes to make our yoke easy
and our burden light.

All Liturgy Is Creative

It is under the sheltering mantle of the Holy Spirit that we
proffer the thesis: All liturgy is, of its nature, creative. That is
to say, all liturgy, of its nature, has the power or quality of
creating; it is productive. The indwelling Spirit has the power
of fashioning and shaping us as the people of God; we who
struggle to establish ourselves as committees would have no
hope of forming ourselves as God's people, save the Spirit who
breathes in us—inspires us to—a life that is pure gift. We
are gathered by and in the power of the Spirit to be nourished
by our communion with one another and the Lord, in the
word and in the bread and cup of life. We do not plan such
encounters but we would do well to prepare for them. Truly
creative liturgy has little to do with novelty or variation in
ritual. If there is any novelty to be considered, it is nothing more
and nothing less than the novelty of how God's Spirit may
choose to move among us in a particular time and place, in a
particular celebration. Such novelty cannot be planned or
designed; it is always a surprise. This is not unrelated to the
surprise of the liturgy team when, after what they have deemed
to be a disastrous celebration, parishioners leave the church
thanking them for a liturgy that truly touched their lives.

The Liturgy Team and Creative Liturgy

Should we then scrap the liturgy team and leave all in the
hands of the Spirit? No! Creative liturgy, as we have defined it,
is precisely the sort of celebration for which the liturgy team
needs to prepare. This is the work of preparing a time and
place, a word and table, a prayer and song that help render the
assembly open and docile to the presence and power of the
Spirit in our midst. From the team's point of view, the task is
to prepare that form of worship that renders the community
vulnerable, as the created, to the Creator. In all of this, the

team must remember that its work will neither guarantee nor ultimately hinder the Spirit's ministry among God's assembled people. A certain humility is in order here, which will serve to lessen any exaggerated sense of responsibility that the team may bear for the community's prayer life.

Creative liturgy is worship born of, sustained by and open to the work of God's Spirit; any other notion of "creative liturgy" misses this primary and primordial mark. Communities that prepare for and celebrate this kind of liturgy will find, at least initially, that worship of this sort is no easy venture. To prepare for celebrations that are creative in that word's truest sense is to approach liturgical prayer with an earnest seriousness and with a patience for the Spirit's moving in our life of prayer. For a while we may pine for the fleshpots of novelty and grumble over our hunger for variation, but one Sunday morning we will gather up the fruits and gifts of the Spirit in our midst and that nourishment will be for us like manna in the desert.

Liturgy Is Productive

The definition of "creative" includes a second entry that also deserves our attention: "productive of." How is liturgy, of its nature, "productive," and what does it produce? To get to the heart of this question, let us listen to a familiar exchange.

> Mary: You know, I just didn't get much out of Mass today.
> John: Well, you get out of Mass what you put into it.

In light of our discussion thus far, what are we to make of Mary's complaint and John's familiar, if not glib, pious response?

What did Mary hope to "get out of Mass" today? What does her desire to "get" something tell us about her approach to her community's prayer? Perhaps it is because we have spoken for too many years of "going to Mass to receive communion" that we have come to expect that the liturgy ought to give us something.[10] Indeed, the liturgy gives us nothing less than God's own word and communion with the Lord and the

Lord's family in prayer and sacrament. Still, the liturgy is not constituted to be some sort of spiritual department store where we go to pick up what we need. The eucharistic liturgy is rooted in the Lord's last supper with his friends, when he offered bread and wine and gave thanks and praise. Our celebration of the eucharist is the remembering and doing of what Jesus did: He gave, and eternally gives, thanks and praise to the Father who, through baptism, opened the gates of everlasting life for the Son and for his brothers and sisters. Liturgy is first and primarily a time for giving, not for getting. As far as we are able, we are thankful that each time we give what is owed the Lord, there takes place a holy exchange of gifts in which the Lord returns to us more than we can dream of offering.

A Holy Exchange of Gifts

At Christmas we are accustomed to exchanging gifts with friends and family. We purchase gifts for others with the knowledge that a gift will in turn be presented to us. But then comes the new friend with whom the custom of exchanging gifts has not been established. Should you offer a gift to such a person in your first Christmastime together? Will your friend be embarrassed if he or she has no gift to return? Throw caution to the wind! You are fond of this person and you want to express your affection with a yuletide offering. Have you known the joy of that experience when, upon presenting your gift, your friend returns the favor? Your new friend's gift was not expected; it was, like yours, pure gift, not a trade-off. Something like this is the holy exchange of gifts shared between Creator and creation in worship.

Now, what of John's response to Mary? At first glance he appears to be on the right track in reminding her that she must "put something into" the liturgy. Unfortunately, there is a commercial equation in John's advice that betrays a consumer mentality: Put something in and you'll get something out; invest and live off the interest.

John's response to Mary is based on an understanding of productivity that does not balance. The relationship between

God and God's people is celebrated and realized in Christian worship. What we "put into" worship is not an investment on which we expect a return. At best, it is partial payment of a debt that leaves us eternally in arrears. If such "productivity" is alien to the dynamic of Christian worship, can it be said that liturgy is "productive"?

What the Spirit Brings Forth

Recalling that liturgy is, of its nature, creative precisely because our worship is the work of God's Spirit, we must ask what it is that the Spirit produces. The same dictionary that defines *creative* as "productive of" defines the verb *produce* in this way:

> produce, *v.t.* (L. *producere,* to bring forward, fr. *pro* + *ducere* to lead) 1. To bring forward; to exhibit; to show; as, to produce a witness in court. 2. a. to bring forth, as young, or as a natural product or growth; to bear; yield.[11]

These are the first definitions of *produce:* financial, manufacturing and theatrical meanings are secondary and tertiary. Once again, the root meaning of a word brings us to the heart of the matter: Liturgy is creative inasmuch as its life force, the Holy Spirit, is productive of our worship and of we who offer it.

The Spirit is "productive" in our divine service as it brings forward, exhibits and shows what is otherwise hidden or ignored. It is the Spirit who opens for us the words of the scriptures and who shows us what is hidden in the gifts we offer. It is the Spirit of truth and justice who opens our eyes to the One who is our saving witness in the court of God's judgment. It is the Spirit who brings us forth as the harvest and yield of that new creation of which Christ is the firstfruits. The Spirit is "productive of" us as the people of God.

It is in this sense that our worship is productive. We can see that this productivity does not depend on some spiritual capital that we might invest. Once again we are reminded that we stand empty-handed before God when we worship. What we have to offer is already God's gift to us; what is brought forth — produced — is our need to give thanks for all we have been given.

Notes

1. It should be acknowledged that in the minds of many observers there is little or no distinction made between these two sets of categories: What is informal is contemporary; what is formal is traditional. This quick pairing of categories of itself is cause for us to investigate the matter.

2. Marty Haugen, "We Remember," (Chicago: GIA Publications, Inc., 1980).

3. Eucharistic Prayer for Reconciliation 1.

4. Suzanne Toolan, "How Brightly Deep" or "The Call," (Chicago: GIA Publications, Inc., 1971).

5. Webster's New World Dictionary of the American Language, (New York: World Publishing Co., 1960).

6. Exsultet.

7. Webster's New World Dictionary of the American Language, (New York: World Publishing Co., 1960).

8. Eucharistic prayers of the Roman Missal.

9. John Foley, SJ, "One Bread, One Body," (Phoenix: North American Liturgy Resources, 1978).

10. Compare with the dynamic of the Liturgy of the Hours as described in Chapter One, p. 23–25.

11. Webster's New World Dictionary of the American Language, (New York: World Publishing Co., 1960).

Chapter 4

LIVING *the* TRADITION: A CONTEMPORARY TASK

M uch of what the contemporary worshiper thinks of as old or "traditional" was once, itself, new and innovative. The process of the new becoming old is ever with us, and our own generation of worship is always leaving its unique mark on the ritual prayer that was handed down to us from our ancestors. This chapter will discuss "traditions" and how they make their way into our community's heritage.

BUILDING CATHEDRALS

The cathedral at Chartres is recognized by many who have never visited France. Picture postcards and photographs in art books have made it a familiar sight. The most breathtaking perspective of this grand house of worship, however, is seen when approaching the small town of Chartres by train or car. Suddenly, out of the simplicity of the French farm country rises this inspiring testimony to the faith of those who lived in another age, in simpler times. One stands in awe.

My visit to Chartres was blessed by two very moving experiences. They may help us look at how "tradition" becomes part of the *tradition* of our worship. Having walked around the interior of the cathedral for about an hour, I sat in a pew to pray. As a visitor, I found that the beauty of the place was more a distraction than an aid to my meditation. One thought was foremost in my mind: This place spanned several hundred years in the building. Generations of craftspeople and their families were born to the building of this church, knowing that they would die long before its completion. Our own age admits of few like experiences. Can we imagine giving our life and trade to a project whose end we will never celebrate? One remembers Moses, who was not permitted to enter into the Promised Land.

Sitting in the cathedral, I looked up to the vaulted ceilings and fine stonework, delicate and majestic in detail. I imagined a stonecutter who may have spent his life working on a dozen carvings to be placed in a wall that would never shelter his prayer.

As I entertained these thoughts, there came music, the voices of singers outside the cathedral, their hymn muffled by the great stone walls. The song and its singers burst through the cathedral doors, and the place was filled with 500 young people who had pilgrimaged from all over France to this small village and its mighty house of prayer. Each parish group in the throng carried its own banner, and these flags punctuated the field of pews in which the pilgrims took their places. The aisles were decorated with mounds of colorful backpacks, resembling bushes with overgrown blossoms. Some musicians gathered behind the presider's chair; a vested priest approached the chair and called the community to prayer in the eucharist. The already kaleidoscopic beauty of the place was refracted a thousand times over by the prism of God's people at prayer.

Generations of Builders

What can the local parish learn from this experience of cathedral worship? We whose ministry attends to the celebration of liturgy are not unlike those whose craft helped the cathedral at Chartres pierce the skies of the French countryside. We are one in a long line of generations past and yet to come whose work is to shape a few of the stones that help build up the temple of God's people at prayer. The names of few among us will be recorded or remembered, but our work is crucial: to make sturdy the foundations, strong the flying buttresses and true the beauty of that shelter which is the liturgy for the hearts of God's people. We must know and trust the work of the generations before us, as surely as the generations to come will need to trust our contribution. We must respect the original plans for the edifice upon which we build. To change the design midway through construction is to weaken what we build and to place undue stress on a structure as delicate as it is strong. We must learn to be content that ours is not the privilege of cementing in the cornerstone; that finishing touch will be accomplished only at the coming of the One who is the cornerstone.

In the meantime, we go about the work that is ours to do. We live and pray in the unfinished shelter that is our inheritance, and we do what we can and must to bequeath to our children the beauty of what we have been given, hoping that we have added to, and never marred, what has been entrusted to our care.

Here Come the Apprentices!

Let us not be surprised, however, when the next generation troops into our shelter, singing its own songs and littering the place with the baggage of its pilgrimage. This is as it should be! These pilgrims are our children in the family of faith. They are the apprentices in our craft. They come not to destroy but to enjoy the beauty of our work! If they appear to be bulls in the china shop, then they are very much like we were in our younger days. How easily and quickly we forget! These are the new builders, and they have as much to learn from us as we have to learn from them. They come with new tools and methods, new insight and depth. In our working with them, the past and the present are wonderfully met, and we find hope that the building will not come to an end. These new workers will make mistakes, and their mistakes will often remind us of our own. Young and old alike, we need to be gentle and reverent towards one another as the heritage is handed on, as the task of Peter and John "preparing a place to celebrate the Passover," is entrusted to new disciples.

The divine service we offer, much like the building of cathedrals, is both a traditional and contemporary task.

A Word to Pilgrims and New Disciples

As the next generation takes up the work of building the temple of God's people at prayer, the temptation to change the plans midstream is great. The newest of ideas often appear to be without fault; time and history teach us a different lesson.

Our liturgical prayer is like a "treasure in clay jars, so that it may be made clear that this extraordinary power belongs to God and does not come from us" (2 Corinthians 4:7). The treasure is one of strength but it must be handled with gentleness, for its true home is the fragile heart of God's people. This treasure is not one to be kept under lock and key. Rather, it is one to be brought out for all to see and to touch, so that we might be touched by it. It is a treasure precisely because it is the communion of God and God's holy people.

We whose ministry is the liturgy do not own this treasure. At best we are guardians or, as the scriptures would put it, servants of this holy ground where Creator and creation are at one. The responsibility is a grave one, and the trust is sacred.

I do not mean, however, that the builders of this generation have nothing to offer for the building-up of this treasure. From our own times and experience the liturgy will be embellished by our artistry. But we must think before we act, and walk before we leap.

NEW "TRADITIONS"

The history of Christian worship is the story of how the disciples of Christ have prayed through the centuries; the story is traced by the mark that each generation makes upon its liturgy. For the most part, the treasure has been passed whole and intact from generation to generation. At times the worship tradition has been scarred or blemished in the process. The signatures of the present age will be many upon our heritage of prayer; we live in a time when a plurality of liturgical expressions struggle to be faithful to the one body we are in Christ. Gone are the days when those who went to Sunday Mass would experience exactly the same liturgy in South Bend, Indiana, in Sydney, Australia, and in a mission chapel in Haiti. Liturgy now bears not only the stamp of the age, but also of each local community, for worship practices and customs vary from parish to parish and, at times, from Mass to Mass within one parish. In the future, students of the liturgy will have vast storehouses of photocopied and quick-printed documentation for their study of worship in late twentieth-century America.

As servants of the liturgy, we are responsible for what we have received from our ancestors in the faith and for what we shall pass on to our children in that same faith. Each generation, then, is a crucial link in that chain of prayer that keeps us united with that Passover prayer of Jesus in an upper room. Our responsibility demands that we take gentle care in how we celebrate the liturgy and how we fashion this inheritance as prayer for our own times. The divine service we offer is the prayer of the ages and the sacrament of the age that is come and yet to come, the reign of God.

We who hold and shape this prayer in the present moment must be familiar with its history and its crucial role in the life of the church. A careful and studied approach is required of those who shape and hand on the heritage of our liturgical prayer. This is as true at the local parish level as it was for the bishops of the Second Vatican Council and continues to be for all national conferences of bishops. To help us to understand what is required in this approach, the following example is offered.

Holding Hands during the Lord's Prayer

In many communities, it has become the practice at eucharist for those present to join hands during the Lord's Prayer. It has become a "tradition," if ten years can be said to constitute a tradition, or at least a custom associated with Mass on the Lord's Day.

Those who encourage this practice tell us that the linking of hands throughout the assembly during the Lord's Prayer helps those present see themselves as one body made up of its many members. It is also suggested that this gesture signifies that we are indeed one family of brothers and sisters whose spiritual kinship in Christ allows us to pray to the God whom we name Our Father.

On the face of things, one can hardly argue with the spirituality offered as justification for this practice: It is Christ-centered and ecclesial. Face-value consideration is not sufficient in this case. The gesture, in some communities, has become part of the ritual prayer of God's people, and it is not a gesture without significance. Holding hands with one's neighbors is not an element of the worship tradition that has been handed down to us, but it is one that may very well pass to the next generation, or to a neighboring parish, as part and parcel of how Christians celebrate the eucharist. The reader may think this a minor point not worth our consideration, but we need to remember that much of our liturgy's reform in the past twenty-five years was the work of discarding those "elements which, with the passage of time, came to be duplicated, or were added [to the rites] with but little advantage" (*Constitution on the Sacred Liturgy,* 50).

How, then, are we to evaluate this custom of holding hands during the Lord's Prayer? We shall look at the origin of the custom, its intended purpose and its placement within the whole liturgical act of the eucharist.

Origin Our experience is that assemblies of worshipers do not spontaneously reach out to take their neighbors' hands when the presider says or sings, "Let us pray with confidence to the Father. . . ." Somewhere along the line, a priest or other minister instructed the people before Mass, or just after the Great Amen, in the meaning of this gesture and invited them to do it. Where the gesture has endured, we can presume that it was initially met with a generally positive response. A few questions come to mind:

- What is to be thought of a gesture or symbol whose meaning needs to be explained to those about to experience it?
- What are the implications of introducing into the people's prayer a gesture that involves the entire assembly but one not generally anticipated to be part of worship in the Roman rite?
- Does the individual worshiper have a legitimate claim in expecting that parish worship will be celebrated according to the liturgical books? What actions might be said to be an infringement on this claim?

Issues Some real issues surround this seemingly simple gesture: Some people simply do not want or do not like to hold hands with their neighbors during the Lord's Prayer. Must they? Should they? In parishes where this is the custom, does the individual worshiper have any options? One can steel oneself against the exchange of the sign of peace, which is a ritual expectation, but one is harder put to break the chain of hand-holding fellowship for the duration of the Lord's Prayer.

And what of the visitor who is not familiar with the version of the Lord's Prayer that is being sung? He or she must either break the chain in order to hold the hymnal in which the music appears or not sing.

And what of the deaf person who prays in sign?

Purpose and Placement If this gesture is intended to help us understand that in worship we are gathered as one people in Christ for the purpose of praising God, our Father, what is to be said of the value and meaning of the opening and communion rites in our celebration of Mass? Are the signs, gestures and songs of the opening and communion rites so weak that they need to be shored up by the addition of this gesture during the Lord's Prayer?

The holding of hands is a gesture added to the many gestures already in the Mass (standing, bowing, genuflecting, processing, making the sign of the cross, exchanging the kiss of peace, giving and receiving of bread and cup). How does this added gesture blend with all the others?

Some argue that the exchange of the kiss of peace is poorly placed in the Roman rite, that it interrupts the flow of the liturgical actions toward the communion procession. The new edition of the sacramentary, which is currently going through the approval process, may allow the sign of peace to be placed elsewhere in the liturgy. Others argue that the Lord's Prayer presents a similar problem and would be better prayed as the conclusion to the General Intercessions. (The new edition of the sacramentary will not offer this as an option.) Does a gesture during the Lord's Prayer help or hinder an already problematic moment? How does the hand-holding custom relate to the kiss of peace? Have we considered the fact that one must drop the hands held in one sign of unity in order to shake hands or embrace in another sign of unity?

Finally Suppose that one day, for whatever reason, it is decided by the presider or the liturgy team that this custom should be discontinued. How can this be accomplished without giving the lingering impression that the Lord's Prayer is no longer a community prayer, but now it is a prayer of individuals? Would the Lord's Prayer seem "less" when restored to its original proportions?

Drawing Conclusions

You will have concluded by now that I am not altogether happy with the custom of holding hands during the Lord's Prayer. You are correct. You should also know that I have ministered in a parish where this practice was the custom in two of our three Sunday assemblies. (Guess: How many "traditional" and how many "contemporary" liturgies were celebrated in this schedule of Masses?) The custom was well in place long before my arrival in the parish, and it continued after I left. I made the effort to honor what is, for many, a meaningful gesture. As much as I would argue against the incorporation of this gesture, much more would I argue against its arbitrary cessation on the word of a newcomer. That is how precious and sacred is the prayer of God's people whom we serve.

All this is by way of example. Questions have been raised to help in discerning the "traditions" that spring up (or are announced) in local communities. Such customs will, for the most part, neither make nor break the community's worship nor provide a new chapter in the history of Christian liturgy. This, however, does not lessen the importance of our shaping the liturgy in local communities, nor does it free ministers and assemblies from the responsibility entrusted to those who are servants of the community and the divine service it offers. We shape our prayer for today with thanksgiving for what we have received and with hope for what we will pass on.

Thank God none of the builders of the cathedral at Chartres had any bright ideas about lowered ceilings or indirect lighting!

Chapter 5

NEGOTIATING *the* RITE

t has been suggested that someone write a book on liturgy "for those who just don't get it." The intention is that such a text might reach those whose liturgical practice betrays a certain ignorance of the history, theology, ritual and documentation that are part and parcel of understanding and celebrating worship in the Roman Catholic tradition. I choose the word "ignorance" carefully, noting that ignorance, although an unhappy judgment, is at least a forgivable offense, whereas the charge of blatant disregard would warrant greater demands on mercy.

LITURGISTS AND TERRORISTS

I am aware that categorizing some as "those who just don't get it" smacks of elitism and hints at a form of liturgical gnosticism. I've already been asked, more often than I care to remember, if I know the difference between a liturgist and a terrorist. The alleged difference is that one can negotiate with a terrorist. Get it? Yes, we all do. But there are some things that some people just don't "get" quite so easily. This chapter addresses these issues.

The liturgist-terrorist joke is clever, but like much humor, it skillfully targets one group and generously spares another. Let me explain. My own experience of liturgists is that they tenaciously hold what they have learned to be the truth about ritual (particularly its history and theology) and offer this as the best footing for understanding the liturgy and for considering any variation, change or development in its celebration. If nothing else, a student of the liturgy understands that worship's history is a story of adaptation, inculturation and growth. In one sense, it is precisely negotiation—the negotiation of differences, developments and departures from the norm—that constitutes a whole strain of the history of ritual. Because liturgists understand the historical development of ritual prayer, they are often among the first to propose a direction that further growth might take. Liturgists are not, by character or training, intransigent guardians of some entrenched status quo.

Perhaps the joke at hand has liturgists confused with rubricists. The rubricist, demanding obsessive fidelity to the letter of the law, is often stubborn and difficult to work with. A kind of fundamentalist, the rubricist tends to see liturgical instructions as ends in themselves, having a life independent of people's prayer, while the liturgist understands the rubrics to be helpful and necessary guidelines. The liturgist understands that the ritual prayer of believers is a reality continually negotiated by the faith of the assembly, the particular joys and sorrows of the worshipers, the distribution of talents, gifts and charisms, and the people's capacity to receive what God's Spirit desires to offer and accomplish through their ritual prayer.

If by negotiation is meant a mutual consideration by two parties of certain facts and options with a view toward legitimate compromise, then I submit that it is the parochial practitioner (pastor, liturgy coordinator, worship team, pastoral musician, parishioners) who is often the less willing to enter into knowledgeable, reasonable debate about liturgical matters. Such people too often and too easily dismiss the "expert" as a purist, a rubricist or as simply "not pastoral." One tires of hearing about solutions to liturgical problems where the "pastoral" response is little more than a thinly disguised rejection of the church's tradition or teaching on a particular issue— often at the expense of worship's integrity.

The liturgy is not some amorphous, free-floating concept waiting to be sketched into reality by a local assembly and its minister. Rather, the liturgy in the Roman Catholic tradition is a theologically grounded enterprise with a documented history. The liturgy is itself a source of theological reflection. The liturgy has its own spirituality rooted in sacred scripture and in the history of our communion. The liturgy's forms and functions (a significant part of our faith's heritage) are clearly spelled out in directives and instructions from legitimate authority on the international, national and diocesan levels. The liturgy is a recognizable, ordered discipline of ritual entrusted to the people of the local church so that they might rightly and justly render to God the thanks and praise which is their duty and their salvation, in communion with the church throughout the world.

The liturgy then, though in one sense negotiated, is never an arbitrary reality. Some liturgical issues admit of no negotiation whatsoever. One cannot negotiate between water and milk as the liquid matter for baptism. The liturgy has muscle and is stretched over a skeleton of defined proportions. It has a history, a purpose and a function. It has survived a good deal of rough handling, because ultimately the liturgy is the work of Christ among us, his body, the church. Because it is the work of Christ, it is deserving of our utmost respect and reverence.

"ONLY CONNECT!"

An insightful essay on contemporary culture raises some important points for this discussion. Michiko Kakutani writes:

> Not so long ago, artists rallied to E. M. Forster's famous imperative, "Only connect"—connect the past and the present, connect the visible and the hidden, connect the dots and find the pattern in the carpet. Today that battle cry has been replaced by a new exhortation: Stop making sense.

In both the highest of highbrow art and the flimsiest of consumer trash, sloppiness has become the style of the day. Not only are old-fashioned stories with beginnings, middles and ends on their way to extinction, but basic principles of dramatization, character and structure are in danger of becoming endangered species as well. Form has been replaced by formlessness on one hand and formula on the other. A result: the proliferation of movies, books and plays that feel either entirely unedited or so schematic that they verge on the absurd.[1]

The essayist is writing about films and novels, and it is not the business at hand to wonder how the same cultural dynamics seem to find expression both in worship and the arts. The parallels, however, are many and interesting.

"Stop making sense!"

I'm not suggesting that parish liturgy teams are crafting processional banners emblazoned with the words "Stop making sense!" As a matter of fact, much of the poor liturgy experienced by our assemblies is the result of efforts to "make sense" of our ritual and the scriptures in the terms and vocabulary of the present moment. It cannot be denied that liturgical celebration and preaching have a responsibility to help the gathered assembly understand and have a sensible, sensate and spiritual experience of the mysteries of salvation in the moment at hand. "*This* is the day the Lord has made! Let us rejoice and be glad!" Some things, however, are better experienced raw than made sense of for us.

The point at which things become nonsensical is the point at which connections fail to be made. When ritual fails to connect the past with the present with the future in the paschal mystery; when liturgy fails to connect the visible and the hidden in the sacramental life of the church; when our community prayer fails to help us "connect the dots" in the saving patterns of life and death larger than ourselves and beyond our immediate experience — when any of this fails to happen, then those responsible for preparing worship and for ministering its celebration have figuratively begun to cut out the felt letters for the "Stop making sense!" banner.

The Presider's Ministry

Let us take the ministry of the ordained presider at Sunday eucharist as an example. We know that "no other single factor affects the liturgy as much as the attitude, style and bearing of the celebrant: his sincere faith and warmth as he welcomes the worshiping community; his human naturalness combined with dignity and seriousness as he breaks the bread of word and eucharist."[2] Many presiders embody this description well; others fail. In all cases, however, it is the presider who must ultimately take responsibility for the way in which his community celebrates the liturgy. He has a unique responsibility for the ritual life of his people.

77

What kind of connections does the presider make? For many years presiders have known and been reminded that their proper greeting of the assembly at eucharist should sound something like, "May the grace and peace of our Lord Jesus Christ, the love of God, and the fellowship of the Holy Spirit be with you all." Study this greeting and note the appropriate connections its graceful and prayerful announcement makes for all present. The greeting itself is filled with the connections of relationship in the Trinity, prayerfully bestowed by the presider upon the people who connect with the presider in their ritual response, "And also with you." Contrast this with, "Good morning, everybody!" (Assembly mumbles, "Good morning, Father.") Father continues, "I'm not sure why the Lord has given us such a rainy weekend, but I hope you're all praying that the weather clears up before the parish picnic this afternoon."

Where do these words lead us? To what and to whom? The presider who begins in this manner is likely to maintain a folksy running commentary throughout the celebration, continually draining the liturgical act of its ritual power. Making connections fuels the liturgical act, while missed connections disable it.

In an effort to be funny or different or casual, a presider was recently heard to replace, "Let us offer each other a sign of the Lord's peace," with "Well, you know what to do now." Suddenly the flow of prayer and action is interrupted and attention is drawn to the presider, whose words were his, not the liturgy's, and who took the gracious invitation of the church's text and made of it his own one-liner. He has disconnected the assembly from the church's ritual prayer and has connected it to himself and his attempt at humor.

It is unlikely that the average parish community consciously experiences a sense of disconnection when this happens, but the cumulative effect over a period of time can be devastating. We often hear the complaint that the "new liturgy" (the liturgy of the postconciliar liturgical books) has lost the sense of mystery that the "old liturgy" had. I suggest that the current liturgy has just as much potential for the experience of mystery as did the old, but two realities have intervened. A liturgy celebrated in a foreign tongue (Latin) and according to a minimalist ritual that few understood produced a very mysterious experience indeed. The introduction of the vernacular and the broader, more substantial strokes of the current liturgical books have a tendency to unveil what before was mysteriously hidden. When what is unveiled is experienced as casual and informal, if not humorous, then the people will experience something less than mystery. It is not the unveiling, the liturgical reform, that has been the problem but what has been exposed in the unveiling. Sooner or later it becomes clear that like the emperor who was in fact not wearing new clothes, many presiders and other ministers are appearing in the sanctuary *sans* vestments! It is not one experience that leads people to this conclusion, but rather the cumulative effect of more than thirty years of experiencing the breakdown of connections in our worship.

However genuine and earnest the intentions may be, efforts at being casual or personal draw attention to the presider, even though the presider's constant task is to draw the attention of the assembly beyond himself to the Lord and

to the many manifestations of the Lord's presence in the liturgical celebration (including the person and ministry of the
presider). In simpler terms, the casual presider tends to make
the wrong connections, or no connections at all. Because
"no other single factor affects the liturgy as much as the attitude, style and bearing of the celebrant," the presider has a
special responsibility for the connections that his presence, his
words and his actions make, or fail to make, in the people's
experience of their prayer.

The Presider and the Liturgy Team

The presider's responsibility extends beyond his presence, gestures and words in the sanctuary. The presider, as the title suggests, has a responsibility for all the ministries in the liturgy
and for how they function and how they enable connections in
the celebration. Just as "no other single factor affects the
liturgy as much as the attitude, style and bearing of the celebrant" in the sanctuary, so might it be said that no single factor affects the preparation for the celebration of the liturgy
outside the sanctuary. Since it is increasingly the case that the
presider is also the pastor (or a member of the pastoral staff), it
is easy to see how his responsibility as presider extends to his
relationship—his connectedness—to the community at large, to
the parish liturgy team and liturgy coordinator, to the greeters,
pastoral musicians, lectors, preachers, ministers of the eucharist, ministers of dance and ministers of Christian initiation. All
of these various ministries are charged, like the presider, with
helping the community to connect: to connect the past with the
present with the future in the paschal mystery; to connect the
visible and the hidden in the sacramental life of the church; and
to "connect the dots" in the saving patterns of life and death
larger than ourselves and beyond our own experience.

Among all the ministries for Sunday eucharist, the liturgy
team has a special role in shaping the prayer of the assembly;
the presider's relationship to this group is therefore of great
importance. The work of the liturgy team has a great influence
on how, or if, the most important connections are made in

the celebration of the people's prayer. The connection between the presider and the liturgy team is essential, and the work that is theirs to do, in common, is the work of negotiation. I do not mean a negotiation between the presider's point of view and the liturgy team's point of view—even though many liturgy team meetings boil down to this unhappy reality. What I do mean is that the presider and the team work together to negotiate the preparations for Sunday eucharist in such a manner that enables the assembly to give the thanks and praise that are their duty and their salvation.

Working together, the presider and team begin with the liturgical books (the calendar, the sacramentary with its General Instruction, the lectionary and other pertinent documents) and begin to prepare for the people's Sunday prayer. If these books and documents are the starting point and guide, then a number of predictions can be made about the shape, style, content and ambience of the community's worship on the Lord's Day:

- The space for worship will be suitably enhanced or simplified according to the demands of the season or feast.
- At all times, and especially in the great cycles of Advent/Christmas and Lent/Easter, all the church's rituals will be celebrated fully, and as indicated by the liturgical books (including, therefore, the rites for the Christian initiation of adults and of children of catechetical age—without exception).
- The procession of ministers at the beginning of Mass will include the cross bearer, acolytes, book bearer and presider.
- The work of lectors, acolytes, deacons and ministers of the eucharist will be carried out by the appropriate ministers, who will have been catechized and prepared for these ministries.
- An entrance song, the responsorial psalm, the gospel acclamation, the Holy, Holy, the memorial acclamation, the Great Amen, the Lamb of God and the communion processional will all be sung.

- The musical repertoire will be scripturally based and will not dominate the liturgical action but will serve it; cantors and choirs will assume their appropriate roles in serving the people's prayer.
- A homily will be preached, and it will be based on the scriptures of the day or on some text from the liturgy, not on any other topics except in such ways as other topics are helpful in preaching the scriptures and bringing their message to the assembly.
- The general intercessions will be both general and intercessory; they will be read or sung by the appropriate minister.
- Communion will be offered under both kinds at every Sunday celebration of the eucharist.
- Any necessary announcements will be made after the prayer after communion and before the blessing and dismissal.

The negotiation of these items is not a matter of "will we or won't we" but is a question of "how will we and when will we?" The liturgy team does not debate whether or not the acclamations will be sung, but it does enter into discussion with the music ministers regarding which musical setting will be sung and when that setting will change on a seasonal or festal basis. The liturgy team does not pick and choose which, if any, of the rites of Christian initiation are to be celebrated, but rather prepares for all of them to be celebrated in their circumstances. The liturgy team does not argue over whether or not Santa Claus will visit the Vigil Mass on Christmas Eve to place the image of the Christ child in the crèche, because it is clear from the ritual books that there is no room in our church's prayer for the introduction of costumed fantasy figures at any time, let alone during the Vigil of the Incarnation celebrating God's very Word taking on human flesh for our salvation. (Arguments may be advanced about Saint Nicholas being the origin of the Santa Claus myth. Legitimate as this may be, it will make little difference to the impressionable children for whom such displays are intended.)

When the liturgy team meets to prepare for worship, it sets
about the work of negotiation within the well-defined boundaries supplied by the liturgical books. As soon as the team
steps outside these boundaries, it courts sloppiness.

The Roman rite in which we worship is lean and clean. It
has about it a restrained modesty which, when respected, allows
it to be a vehicle of praise, lament, joy, sorrow, peace, grief,
happiness, supplication, contrition, healing, adoration and salvation. The scriptures, the ritual of the church's sacramental
life and the song of the church's prayer are the channels through
which all of this life and energy flow.

Sloppy liturgy happens when the basic principles of ritual prayer are unknown, misunderstood or cast aside. Sloppy
liturgy happens when zeal for one cause or another, ignoring
the true character of the Roman rite, uses the liturgy as a
mere prop for its own agenda rather than allowing it to flex
its muscularity in ways appropriate to itself. Sloppy liturgy
happens when the ancient and obvious structures of our rite
are discarded, in whole or in part, in favor of imported structures that add nothing to the integrity of the liturgical act
but in fact detract from it. As Kakutani writes, "Sloppiness
has become the style of the day."

The risk here is more than sloppiness. The endangered
species is not tidiness, but the rite itself. One hears the complaint: "Everywhere you go the liturgy is different. It's not like
the old days when worship was the same in every place."
Of course it's different! It always was. It should be. It must be.
It is. It will be. We sometimes have romantic notions that in
the preconciliar church, Sunday Mass was just the same at
Saint Patrick's Cathedral in New York City as it was in a mis-
sionary's lean-to sanctuary in Africa or a small church in Korea.
This, of course, was not the case, despite the many similari-
ties. Worship is always as different as the worshipers who are
worshiping—and as uniform as the ritual in which they worship! But once we begin to ignore the principles, character
and structure of the rite—to ignore such simple things as the

common sense of the liturgy, its beginnings, its middles and its ends—then we will find that "form has been replaced by formlessness on one hand and by formula on the other." To paraphrase Kakutani, the result is a proliferation of liturgies that feel either entirely unedited or so schematic that they verge on the absurd.

Theme Liturgies If any or all of this seems overdrawn, then I ask you to consider the phenomenon of so-called "theme liturgies." The term may be passé, but its dynamic still fuels the engines of many liturgy teams on a weekly, festal or seasonal basis. The liturgy of our rite resists themes. If there is any theme to our worship, it is the mystery of the death and resurrection of Jesus Christ for our salvation. Period. Within that mystery we lift up our concerns, our needs, our hope and our joy; and always, we are offering praise and thanks to God the Father, through Christ his Son, in the power of the Holy Spirit. To create themes beyond this central mystery is to abandon the inherent form of Christian worship; where more and more extraneous additions are admitted into the liturgy, formlessness threatens. Some of what is admitted is accepted as so compelling that it becomes institutionalized by the local assembly and becomes part of the formula of worship for that community. In too many instances, we find ourselves at worship somewhere between a rite that is so unedited as to be formless or so schematic as to be formulaic. This is as absurd and sloppy—and dangerous—in the arena of ritual prayer as it is in Kakutani's field of films and novels.

THE CONTROLLED EXERCISE OF ART

Does this mean that slavish attention to rubrics is the only path to follow? No, but something else is required.

Decades ago, pioneering modernists from Eliot and Joyce to de Kooning and Picasso created an elliptical art that reflected a dissonant vision. Unlike many of today's artists, these modernists were classically trained: Their art of elision and abstraction was actually a highly controlled exercise; their rebellion rooted in a knowledge of tradition.

Certainly it's easier to never bother acquiring these skills to begin with, and that's exactly what later generations of modernists and post-modernists have done, spilling out their thoughts and feelings without pausing to learn technique. This "whatever" approach to art is happily ratified by our society today — a society conditioned by 24-hour news and TV talk shows to prize immediacy and self-esteem over discipline and craft.[3]

In too many communities, it seems that this "whatever" approach to the art of liturgy is alive and well. What is at work here is a ride on the pendulum, still swinging away from the strictly enforced confines of liturgical law prior to the Second Vatican Council and toward the opposite extreme of "anything goes." The "anything goes" attitude allows for a plethora of abuses:

- "Anything goes" in the parish that refuses to invite the catechumens to be dismissed after the Sunday homily but has no problem with inviting Santa Claus to Christmas Mass.
- "Anything goes" in the parish that continues to withhold the cup from the assembly and insists on offering communion only in the form of consecrated hosts stored in the tabernacle.
- "Anything goes" in the parish "Family Mass" where texts, prayers, gestures and song are reduced to childish levels, ignoring the clear intention of *Directory for Masses with Children*.
- "Anything goes" in the parish where homilies are dispensed with during the heat of summer.
- "Anything goes" in the parish where sacred song is still thought of as icing on the liturgical cake.
- "Anything goes" in the parish where the presider offers a running commentary on the texts and gestures of the liturgy, reducing the whole experience to a weekly catechesis on what he thinks the liturgy should be.

- "Anything goes" in the parish where the rituals of Lent, Palm Sunday and the Triduum are condensed or dispensed with in the name of efficiency.

The art of negotiating in preparing for the celebration of the liturgy is, like all art, a highly controlled exercise. Knowledge of the tradition is crucial, as is knowledge of the history, the theology and the spirituality of worship in our rite. It is much easier not to bother to acquire this knowledge to begin with, however, to begin with less than some mastery of these areas is like walking into an operating room to do surgery with first-aid training as your only qualification. In the sanctuary of prayer, the spiritual life of God's people, their "duty and their salvation" is on the line.

Ignorance Is Not Bliss

Must everyone be an expert? Of course not. Must someone on the liturgy team have a substantial understanding of and respect for the liturgy? Definitely. Must all who are involved recognize the liturgical books as the absolute and ultimate guides for preparing for worship? Most assuredly. This chapter began with a discussion of ignorance. Ignorance can kill in the operating room. Ignorance at the liturgy team meeting can have a lethal effect, too, on the spiritual lives of worshipers. These are strong words and strong charges. In Chapter 2 of this book I wrote of violations of God's holy presence and crimes against those who gather to celebrate that saving presence. When one considers what is "on the table" at the liturgy, there seems to be no term too strong in defense of the liturgical act and those who celebrate it.

And those who "just don't get it?" I don't know if these pages will help or not. I do know that writing them has been helpful for me. Having been actively involved in liturgy for over 30 years, I blush when I remember some of the things I did and sang in the name of liturgical reform! I have made just as many mistakes as the next liturgist, and I am sure that I have sometimes played the part of the terrorist. I know that I must continually challenge myself as well as others to avoid the "whatever" approach to the liturgical arts; to be careful that not just "anything goes" in the community of prayer entrusted to my ministry as pastor and presider; to prepare for all celebrations of the liturgy the hard way — by constant recourse to the scriptures, the tradition and the liturgical books of the church in which I serve.

So, I urge you as I urge myself and the people of my parish: Connect — only connect. Connect the past with the present with the future in the paschal mystery; connect the visible and the hidden in the sacramental life of the church; and "connect the dots" in the saving patterns of life and death larger than ourselves and beyond our own experience. To connect in this fashion is to practice an art, to be faithful to tradition and to serve God's people well. Anything less is a cheap imitation.

Notes

1. Michiko Kakutani, "Stop Making Sense: from High Art to Low, Craft is Becoming Extinct—and No One Seems to Care," *The New York Times Magazine*, June 30, 1996, 18.

2. *Music in Catholic Worship*, 21.

3. Kakutani, *op. cit.*

Chapter 6

SPIRITUALITY *and* LITURGICAL MINISTRY

A
ny discussion of liturgical ministry is incomplete without attention to the interior attitudes the minister
brings to the ministry. This chapter is concerned with
spirituality and the liturgical ministries, including the ministry
of the assembled believers whom other ministers serve. The
broader context for our spirituality of liturgical ministry will
be the experience of intimacy, and the desire for it, in our
worship life.

SPIRITUAL INTIMACY

When we speak of intimacy in this context, we do not mean
spatial or stylistic notions of intimacy in the worship environment or experience. Our concern is, rather, with the spiritual
intimacy that is more an affair of the heart than of ambience.
Spiritual intimacy may be supported by a particular environment or worship style, but it does not root itself in anything save
the encounter with our gracious, loving and merciful God.
Perhaps it is for this reason that the faithful elders in our communities, steeped in years of prayer and devotion, often adapt
more easily to ritual and environmental change than do their
middle-aged offspring. Our elders root their faith in their experience of a faithful and saving Lord rather than in the trappings
that adorn the community's celebration of that salvation.

The spiritual intimacy of liturgical prayer is born of those moments that we call conversion, the turning of our hearts to the God who made us, who redeems us and who sustains us. We speak here of those face-to-face and heart-to-heart moments when the Lord's presence in our lives is unmistakable, unavoidable and deeply powerful. For some these moments are few, but they are not forgotten. This experience of intimacy marks the difference between knowing about God and knowing God.

Worship Nourishes Intimacy

The liturgy does not so much produce or "confect" such moments as much as it nourishes and sustains them. The power of God's love is not confined to or restricted by the celebration of liturgical acts. Indeed, it is this spiritual intimacy that draws us to divine service; it is the prior relationship upon which liturgy thrives. The best example of this is the catechumenate: The celebration of baptism is the sacramental and communal culmination of the work that the Lord began in the hearts of the neophytes long before they were admitted to the communion of the Lord's table. Worship does not invent spiritual intimacy; it sustains and nourishes it.

This is not to downplay the power of the liturgical act in our individual and communal intimacy with the One who dwells in unapproachable light. In the Christian scheme of things, the sacraments and the Liturgy of the Hours are the foremost moments when God's people gather to remember, to find present again and to celebrate the saving deeds of the Lord in our midst. The intimacy between Creator and creation in Christ knows its fullest expression in the church, the assembly of believers. Parted from the work and prayer of the church community, the believer is like the branch cut from the vine, left to wither and die.

There is the story of the preacher who asked his congregation to not worry so much about the salvation of their individual souls but to imagine that they would be called to account as a parish on Judgment Day. Said the preacher, "If you live as a people who are to be judged, you will have no need to worry about yourselves." This preacher helps us put spiritual intimacy into the context of the community's life and worship.

Intimacy and Maturity

It is in the intimacy of communion with other believers that we come to know the height and depth of God's love. Our individual intimacy with the Lord is brought to full growth in the church community; without the community's support and fellowship, we are undernourished. Spiritual intimacy with the Lord yearns to express and share itself with others, for the Lord's intimacy with each of us draws us into that people named as the Lord's beloved. True spiritual intimacy comes to maturity in the assembly, the work and the life of God's people. It was through the people of Israel that the Lord was first revealed, and it is the beloved people of the new Israel who are saved in the mystery of Jesus' dying and rising. "You shall be my people and I will be your God." (Ezekiel 36:28)

Keeping the Law

The intimacy of which we speak is as inescapable as the Lord who calls us to it. The divine Lover who pursues and seduces us will not easily be put off. The embracing arms that seek us out are wide with mercy and strong with compassion. A look at the gospel shows that these same arms welcomed every sinner and outcast imaginable. A singular departure from this is the Lord's reaction to those who used the Law and its ritual not to free people but to hold them bound, to load on their backs burdens too heavy to carry, burdens that they themselves would not lift a finger to ease. In particular, table and Sabbath laws were the downfall of those who could not see beyond the power of structure and style. We who study and exercise the law of ritual in our own times would do well to study Jesus' response in these situations and his approach to the laws that some so "religiously" kept.

Worship both demands of us this inescapable intimacy with the Lord and calls us to it. The intimacy of divine service requires that we be honest as we stand as worshipers before the Lord who made and saves us. In prayer we find ourselves in the light of the One who is all truth, who searches our heart—the heart of who we are as God's people—and knows our every secret. When we gather for worship, the heart of who we are as a community is laid bare for the Lord and all of us to see. A married couple may hide their problems from the sight of all, and even from themselves, but these problems cannot escape revelation in the intimacy of their conjugal relationship. In much the same way, the hidden sins of each community may be closeted for six days of the week, but come the intimacy of Sunday worship, these problems will reveal themselves in a myriad of ways, in the Sunday assembly. Our sins of neglect, of infighting of pettiness and jealousy, of anger and resentment and division—all of these are laid bare and made public as we process to that reconciling table of the eucharist, knowing deep within us how great is our need for the Lord's mercy in our parish family.

A Fellowship of Redeemed Felons

Those charged to preach the gospel in our assemblies have an awesome task indeed. Nothing less than the preaching of the gospel will bring us to acknowledge both our sin and our need to be renewed by that intimacy that only the Lord's mercy can establish. We need to learn to leave our gifts at the altar and to go first to be reconciled with our brothers and sisters. As a people, the intimacy we share is the intimacy of felons who have been pardoned by the world's Judge. Through, with and in the company of our sinless brother, who was judged and executed as a felon for our sake, we offer praise and thanks for the great deeds the Lord has done for us. Pardoned and rejoicing, we are sent forth to minister the mercy of such intimacy with our brothers and sisters.

A SPIRITUALITY FOR
LITURGICAL MINISTERS

Not too long ago, ministry was understood to be the business of bishops, priests and those in religious life. All other work in, for and related to the church was done under the title "lay apostolate." It was also not too long ago that we discovered that ministry was everywhere and it belonged to everyone. We learned, at last, that ministry is the work appropriate to all who are baptized in the mystery of Christ Jesus: "If we have died with Christ, we believe that we are also to live with him" (Romans 6:8), and if we are to live with him, then we are also to work with him.

We speak of the "ministry of the baptized" as the primordial Christian ministry. In the celebration of baptism, the one who anoints and seals with the gift of the Holy Spirit addresses these words to the neophytes:

> My dear newly baptized, born again in baptism, you have become members of Christ and of his priestly people. . . . The promised strength of the Holy Spirit, which you are to receive, will make you more like Christ and help you to be a witness to his suffering, death and resurrection. It will strengthen you to be active members of the church and to build up the Body of Christ in faith and love.
> (*Rite of Christian Initiation of Adults*, 229)

Moments after we are born again in the waters of baptism, we are charged to take up the priestly ministry of Jesus. We are named as witnesses to the whole of Christ's paschal mystery: his suffering, dying and rising.

Each of the Baptized Is Called

How we live out this ministry of the baptized is in some ways the same for all of us and in some other ways different for all of us. The sameness consists in the work of all Christians to give thanks and praise to God for all that is given us, especially for that justice which is ours in Christ. We live out our thanksgiving by doing the work of justice in our communities, our nation and in the world. The difference lies in how each of the baptized is called by God. Many are called to the unique and intimate ministry of married life. Others are called to a single life marked by a freedom to minister in many ways. Some are called to vowed life in a community of ministry. Still others are called to the ministry of sacramental leadership in community and in prayer. But in all of these, baptism is the sacrament that brands the individual as one who shares in the Lord's ministry.

Particular Ministries

In addition to these four major vocational ministries, there is a variety of particular ministries in the life of the church. Indeed, there is a tendency in our own times to name every task a ministry. Consider those communities that have dubbed their refreshment committee "the coffee and doughnuts ministry." In a community where every activity is called a ministry, the term can become so vague as to be meaningless.

This is not to deny that the whole church and all of its life are ministerial realities and that each of the baptized is charged with the ministry of living a gospel life. But when we speak of "ministers," that is, individuals or groups set apart for the service of others, then we must distinguish between those who serve and those who are served. The whole church community thrives on a network of ministries. Those in one ministry serve their brothers and sisters in another, who in turn serve those who serve them. Such complementarity is the genius of our life together.

Why the Rush?

The caution about naming every task a "ministry" comes from a wariness of any neoclericalism that may be afoot on the holy ground of our life with God. Perhaps the language is already too strong, but one wonders why we scramble to anoint all persons and tasks as ministers and ministries. Might we not puzzle over the fact that the ranks of the liturgical ministries tend to fill up much more quickly than the ranks of the justice and peace ministries?

For our purposes here the focus is on those ministries that attend our worship life. There is a certain ambiguity about these servant tasks, and this ambiguity deserves our attention.

Can you think of any other situation, event or community where

- the servants make a grand entrance?
- the servants' names are printed in a program that refers to the invited guests as "All"?
- the servants are guaranteed seats at the head table or in the front rows?
- the servants are the most visible and distinguished individuals?
- the servants are often seen and heard?
- the servants are the first to be served from the banquet table?
- the servants are the first to leave?

The Temptation of Power

Ambiguity abounds here, and the potential for misunderstanding is as wide as the space in which these ministers serve, as long as the aisle down which they process and as close as an apple dangling at arm's length from a tree in the middle of an ancient garden. Our first parents reached not merely for a piece of fruit, but for the power promised in its picking. The serpent had assured them that if they ate the fruit of this tree they would be like gods.

The ambiguity that surrounds the public service of the liturgical minister is ripe with temptation. As vice is often virtue run amok, so the minister's temptation to take power and prestige is often service seduced by the desire to be served. We call this *sin*. We can begin to see how great a need there is for understanding spirituality in liturgical ministry.

MINISTRIES AND SPIRITUALITIES

The proliferation of "ministries" in our church is equalled only by its complement of supporting "spiritualities." Thus we read of a spirituality for lay ministry, a spirituality for the ordained ministries, a spirituality for social justice ministry — the list goes on, though we have yet been spared a "spirituality for the coffee and doughnuts ministry."

What we have said thus far about ministry prompts us to take a careful look at this plurality of spiritualities. If Christian ministry is, at the core, a baptismal ministry, does it not follow that a spirituality for ministry is, at the core, a baptismal spirituality?

The baptismal share in the paschal ministry of Christ calls the individual to surrender his or her talents to the service of the baptized community. For example, the ministry of the pastoral musician is rooted not in the singing of one's song or in the playing of one's instrument, but in the musician's share in the dying and rising of Christ. The spirituality of the pastoral musician flows, then, not from the particular service rendered God's people in the liturgy, but from the musician's share through baptism in the service Christ rendered us in the great paschal liturgy of his dying and rising. The difference in each case is that the particular ministry and its spirituality are expressions of Christ's ministry and spirituality that belong to and oblige the Christian through baptism.

We press this point for two reasons:

1. Ministry and spirituality rooted in baptism are of their nature always subject to the dying and rising of Jesus and therefore subject to the church that is his body.
2. Ministry and spirituality rooted not so much in baptism but in a particular expression of baptismal commitment run the risk of segregation from the community they want to serve and from the broader gospel mission of that community.

To understand the risk in the second reason we will need to appreciate the value in the first.

A Baptismal Spirituality

Spirituality can be defined as the art and discipline of presence to the sacred. This includes, but is so much more than, the quiet intimacy with God that one might experience in prayer or on retreat. The notion of "presence to the sacred" is radically transformed in the paschal mystery of Jesus. God's word become flesh for our salvation and renders sacred the whole of creation; to be present to all that is sacred is to be enmeshed with it, as Jesus in his suffering and dying was enmeshed with our humanity. A baptismal spirituality, then, brands and heals us with the sign of the cross, the tree of new life. The fruit of the tree in Eden provided a temptation to grasp for power. The harvest of the new creation is ours in Christ, surrendered and emptied for our sake. Though we are bathed in the light of the resurrection, our lives and ministry stand always in the shadow of the cross. To paraphrase the psalmist, "in the shadow of your wings, we sing for joy" (Psalm 62).

A baptismal spirituality is one that renders us present to

- the mystery of Jesus dying and rising in our lives
- the Spirit who moves our hearts to prayer
- the presence of the Risen Christ in his body
- the whole of creation, which cries out to be reverenced
- the poor and oppressed, on whose behalf we empty ourselves in the work of justice
- the mercy of God that is our peace and our integrity.

"Let the same mind be in you that was in Christ Jesus, who, though he was in the form of God, did not regard equality with God as something to be exploited, but emptied himself, taking the form of a slave, being born in human likeness." (Philippians 2:5–7) This is the spirituality of God's Servant and of God's servants. We do not live as our own masters and we do not die as our own masters, for while we live we are responsible to the Lord and when we die we die as the Lord's servants (cf. Romans 14:7–9).

Just as worship is our most honest stance before God, so baptism discloses the truth of our relationship with God in Christ and orients us to that ministry which is the Servant's and the servants'. Baptism and the spirituality we draw from it are always ecclesial, communal affairs. Though it is the individual who is plunged into the waters of baptism to die with Christ, it is into the waiting embrace of the baptized community that the individual rises with Christ. From that moment on, the individual ceases to live in isolation. The baptized are enmeshed with Christ's body, the church, and the mesh is one of mutual service.

In short, the value of a baptismal spirituality is its fidelity to the saving ministry of Jesus, which constitutes us as the redeemed and redeeming community.

Spiritualities of Later Origin

Ministries and spiritualities rooted not so much in baptism but in a later, particular expression of baptismal commitment run the risk of segregation from the community to be served and from that community's broader gospel mission. These spiritualities of later origin justify and support particular ministries within the life of the community. Such spiritualities are valuable insofar as they spring from a baptismal spirituality, because the particular ministry in question springs from the baptismal ministry.

The problem arises when the particular expressions of our common baptismal ministry seem to separate us into ministries of greater and lesser importance, value and esteem. What we easily lose sight of is that all ministry is important, valuable and esteemed precisely because it is a share in the Lord's ministry. Ministries are different in kind, but they are equal in value because it is the same Lord who calls each of us to service.

> I do not want you to be uninformed [about spiritual gifts]. There are varieties of gifts but the same Spirit; there are varieties of services but the same Lord; there are varieties of activities but it is the same God who activates all of them in everyone. To each is given the manifestation of the Spirit for the common good. . . . All these are activated by one and the same Spirit who allots to each one individually just as the Spirit chooses.
>
> (1 Corinthians 12:1, 4–7, 11)

Let us use again the example of the pastoral musician. The value of one's ministry in music lies not in the song one sings nor in the gifts that enable one to sing it well. Rather, the value lies in the fact that it is the Lord's song that is sung and that its singing is offered as service by the musically gifted to the community that assembles to join in the Lord's singing. Similarly, a spirituality of music ministry is rooted primarily in the pastoral musician's being fully present to the sacred as it is revealed in the musician's heart, in the self-giving of the musician's offering and in the community through which the musician offers back to God, with thanksgiving, the gifts received.

A spirituality for pastoral musicians and all liturgical ministries involves the emptying out of self-interest and self-esteem—dying to oneself—so that one may offer to the community what belongs to it. My gifts are not mine to give; they belong to the community that calls them forth for the service of God's people. This is how deeply we are enmeshed by baptism in the lives of our brothers and sisters. We are called to live as the community described in the Acts of the Apostles: to be of one heart and one mind, none of us claiming anything as our own, rather, letting everything be held in common (see Acts 4:32).

The danger in the spirituality that evolves from the particular expression of Christian ministry is its tendency to focus and even isolate the minister in that expression. When we name the gifts and the gifted, we must always take care to name the Giver and to be explicit about for whom the gifts are given. Ministers who "stake a claim" on their ministry need to remember that the territory has already been deeded to God's people at prayer. My gifts are not mine to give!

Finally, ministry and spirituality of later origin than that of the baptismal font risk segregation from the broader gospel mission of the community served. This kind of segregation is revealed when, for example, parish musicians are unfamiliar with or not interested in the work of the parish justice and peace committee. A few observations:

- It is not expected that everyone be part of every ministerial effort in a parish community.
- There are, however, elements of parish life and ministry deserving of the attention, interest and support of all the baptized.
- The works of justice, reconciling, care for the poor, hospitality and prayer are the mission of the whole community and of its individual members.
- Some in the community are called to leadership in these gospel-missioned works, but the work of the gospel cannot be confined or consigned to the community's leadership. A working committee does not free the community at large from the work of that committee.
- A community of persons enmeshed in the mystery of Jesus will discover that its several ministries offer the fullest service when they are understood to be complementary and interdependent.

This interdependent complementarity is not simply a coincidence; it is so because the work of all parish ministries (including those who serve the coffee and doughnuts) is one work, and it is one because it is the Lord's!

Liturgy and the Work of Justice

Earlier in this chapter it was noted that the ranks of the liturgical ministries fill up much more quickly than do the ranks of the peace and justice ministries. This imbalance is one that should cause us concern. We have much work to do in reminding ourselves that the Sunday assembly for eucharist is validated or falsified by how the community's ritual translates itself into the work of the reign of God through the week. The community that roots itself in a baptismal ministry and spirituality can never dispense itself from the work of justice, peace or of reconciliation.

Each Sunday we pray in the Preface, "It is right to give him thanks and praise . . . we do well always and everywhere to give you thanks," a translation of *Dignum et justum est. . . vere dignum et justum est, aequum at salutare nos tibi semper at unique gratias agere. . . .* It is unfortunate that the Latin *justum* (just) was lost in the translation. The members of the liturgy committee, the justice and peace committees and the whole assembly of the baptized would be well served in hearing and praying each week this intimate connection between the work of worship and the work of justice. The connection is, in reality, a unity, because the work of liturgy and the work of justice are the work of the Lord. They are our work, too, because we have been invited to "do this in memory" of the Lord.

Chapter 7

REFLECTIONS FOR
LITURGICAL MINISTERS

The reflections in this chapter are offered under the titles of those who prepare for and minister within the liturgy of Sunday eucharist. We name the "gifts and the gifted" not to segregate them but, rather, to help us see how the many members are one body in the Giver of the gifts. Resist the temptation to skip to the section that refers to the service you offer, but read through the whole.

We begin with a reminder from Saint Paul:

> If then there is any encouragement in Christ, any consolation from love, any sharing in the Spirit, any compassion and sympathy, make my joy complete: be of the same mind having the same love, being in full accord and of one mind. Do nothing from selfish ambition or conceit, but in humility regard others as better than yourselves. Let each of you look not to your own interests, but to the interests of others.
>
> (Philippians 2:1–4)

THE MINISTRY OF THE ASSEMBLY

Yours is a share
in the work of the Spirit
of all that is holy,
for in who you are
and in what you do
is found the most powerful experience of the sacred.
Yours is the kingdom community
whose very assembling
is sacrament of God's presence in the world.
In the living words, gestures, sacrifice and meal
of your common prayer,
the living God is disclosed
as the faithful and redeeming Lord
whose tent is pitched among us.[1]

Yours is to be nothing more and nothing less
than the body of Christ.
Yours is the ministry of being
the beloved and espoused of God.
Through your lives and in your midst
the tidings of salvation are faithfully proclaimed.
Yours is the work of telling and handing on
the story of God's mercy.
You are the people
who embody the promise of life forever.
For the world you are evidence
that the word of judgment is tempered with compassion.

Yours is the ministry
of celebrating again and again
the Passover meal of the new Covenant.
Your sacrifice of praise
is a hymn to the Lamb of God
who takes away the sins of the world.
Yours is the work
of gathering at the table

that welcomes all
who turn their hearts back to God.
Yours is the ministry
to bring bread and wine,
to give thanks,
to break and share the bread,
to bless and share the cup —
remembering Christ Jesus broken and poured out
for your sake.
Yours is the proclamation of the *mysterium fidei*,
the mystery of faith.

Come to your ministry from your personal prayer:
It is the home from which you journey
to the house of God's people,
to the tables of their common prayer.
Come prepared to be surprised
by God's word and presence
in the assembly of your neighbors.
Come as you are!
Come as sinners who need to find mercy,
as the redeemed who need to give thanks.
Come with all that needs to be healed,
to the Lord who comes to heal you.
Come with no expectations
but the sure hope of communion with the Holy One
in the family of God's people.

If your community's liturgy is alive and beautiful,
take care lest you begin to worship your worship:
This is idolatry.
If your community's liturgy needs help — offer it!
Model your community's liturgy on Christ's divine service,
not on the experience of neighboring parishes.
The liturgy your parish offers
is a mirror of the life your parish lives:
Look into that mirror and see what you will see;
then do what must be done.

When visitors praise and thank you
for the worship you have offered,
take delight in the blessing they have received,
and rejoice in the work
the Lord has accomplished through you.
Be faithful in the work you do,
for through it the Lord saves his people.

Yours is a share
in the work of the Lord's Spirit
who calls God's people to prayer.
You help prepare the way of the Lord
who comes with mercy and with peace.
Yours is the guardianship of that holy ground
where God and God's people
meet and sit at a common table.
Yours is the work
of preparing the table of the Lord
who is our Passover.
Yours is the task
of calling others to serve at that table,
and of preparing them to serve
with grace and reverence.
Yours is the task
of helping God's people
to shape a prayer that they might sing from their hearts.
Yours is nothing less
than the responsibility of ensuring that
God's word is proclaimed
clearly and with conviction.

Come to your work from your personal prayer;
begin your work together with prayer in common.
Let your meetings be long enough
to do the work that is yours to do,
but not so long as to go beyond where the Spirit leads you.
Root your meetings in the scriptures
of the liturgy you prepare,
for the prayer of that celebration
will be rooted in God's word.
Let your meetings be marked
by a unity in spirit and in ideals.
As others are called by the Lord,
invite them to join in your work.

Remember that the treasure
of the prayer of God's people
is one you hold in an earthen vessel.
Be gentle, and reverence what is entrusted to you.
Let this treasure bear the imprint of your community,
but take care lest it be smudged by your fingers.
Should your zeal sometime
mar or crack this treasure,
do not panic.
Acknowledge and study the error,
remembering that the Lord will heal
what you have broken;
learn, as we all do, from your mistakes.

When your brothers and sisters
thank and praise you for your work,
take delight in a prayer that has touched their hearts,
and rejoice in the work
the Lord has accomplished through you.
Be faithful in the work you do,
for through it the Lord saves his people.

THE MINISTRY OF HOSPITALITY

Yours is the first
of Christ's faces to greet God's people
as they assemble for prayer.
Your greeting of welcome
is the first wish that "The Lord be with you!"
Yours is the word
that welcomes the stranger to be at home,
or the silence
that makes of our assembly a foreign land.
Yours is the task of discretion:
knowing how to welcome,
and when and where to seat the latecomer.
Yours may be the last word
that ushers the community
to its week of work
in the Lord's vineyard.
Yours is the Lord's face and voice
for those who enter and depart
the holy ground of prayer.

Come to your work and your post from your personal prayer;
be as ready as the Lord to meet his people.
Let your welcome and your smile be for all who enter;
remember that you will have time
to see your close friends later in the week.
Seek out the lost and the confused;
do not wait for them to come to you.
When appropriate,
lend a hand and an arm to the disabled,
remembering your own infirmities.
Greet each person as the Lord,
for that is precisely whom you meet.
When taking up the collection,
remember that it is for the work of God's people,
especially among the poor;

remember, too, that many who make an offering
are themselves the poor.

Remember that you stand at the temple gates:
Some will come rejoicing,
and others in fear;
some will come healed,
and others to seek that healing.
Be sensitive, and welcome all as best you can.
Some will rush by and ignore you:
Let go of your disappointment
and pray for the Lord's gentle touch
on their heavy or hurried hearts.
Some may fall ill while at prayer:
See to their needs as you would have them see to yours.
Be slow to judge those who leave early:
Be glad that they have shared in our prayer
and recall that only the Lord
knows the reasons of the heart.

When your brothers and sisters
thank and praise you for your work,
take delight in the welcome they have found,
and rejoice in the work
the Lord has accomplished through you.
Be faithful in the work you do,
for through it the Lord saves his people.

THE MINISTRY OF MUSIC

Yours is a share
in the work of the Lord's Spirit
who draws us together into one,
who makes harmony out of discord,
who sings in our hearts
the lyric of all that is holy.
Yours is the joy of sounding that first note
which brings the assembly to its feet,
ready to praise God.
Yours is to impart
a "quality of joy and enthusiasm
[that] cannot be gained in any other way."[2]
Yours is a ministry
that reaches the deepest recesses
of the human heart;
your work is soul-stirring.
Yours is none other than the Lord's song;
you draw us into that canticle of divine praise
sung throughout the ages in the halls of heaven.[3]
You help us to respond to God's word,
to acclaim the gospel,
to sing of our salvation in Christ.
Yours is a ministry
that gathers our many voices
into one grand choir of praise.

Come to your work from your personal prayer.
Let your rehearsals begin with prayer in common.
Let your practice be marked
by unanimity in spirit and in ideals.
Be gentle in correcting one another:
The kingdom will not fall on a flatted note.
Open your choir to those
whom the Lord has blessed with musical gifts;
help the not-so-gifted discern the talents that are theirs.
Rehearse the Lord's song with the reverence it is due.

Take care to study the scriptures
for the liturgy in which you will serve;
know well the word that calls forth our praise.
Let the lyrics of your songs
be strong, true and rooted in the scriptures;
those who sing the Lord's word sing the Lord's song.
Make no room for the trite, the maudlin, the sentimental.
Open your hearts and voices
to new songs
worthy of God's people at prayer.
Let your repertoire change as all living things must,
but not so much that the song of God's people is lost.

Be ambitious for the higher gifts,
but not beyond your gifts;
respect the range of talent
the Lord has given you and your community.
Think first of the assembly's song,
for this is the song you serve.
Let your music be always
the servant
of the Lord,
of God's people,
of the divine service they offer.
Let the service of your music
complement but never overshadow
the people's ritual prayer.
Let your performance become a prayer,
and your art a gift.
Let technique become no idol,
but a tool for honing the beauty of your gift.

Remember that your ministry
is ever an emptying out of yourself;
when the solo is assigned to another,
let that singer's offering become your prayer.
When no one comments on the new motet,

be thankful that your work
led the people to God, not to you.
When the assembly will not sing,
be patient with them and with yourselves;
the Lord's song is sometimes a quiet one
and silence precedes every hymn.
Waste no time wondering,
"Do you think they liked it?"
but ask at all times,
"Did it help them and all of us to pray?"
When your ministry leads you to music,
it has led you astray.
When your ministry leads you to the Lord,
it has brought you home.

When your brothers and sisters
thank and praise you for your work,
take delight in the song their prayer has become,
and rejoice in the work
the Lord has accomplished through you.
Be faithful in the work you do,
for through it the Lord saves his people.

THE MINISTRY OF PRESIDERS

Yours is a share
in the work of the Lord's Spirit
who gathers us from east to west
to make an offering of praise
to the glory of God's holy name.
Yours is the task of calling us
to remember God's mercy
and our need for it.
Yours is the voice that calls us
to hear God's holy word,
and to share in the meal of the Lord's supper.
You "collect" our many prayers
and make them one in our prayer as church.
With us, and in our name,
you take bread and wine,
you speak our thanks to God,
break the bread of life
and bless the cup of salvation.
Yours is to preside
over the great thanksgiving of God's people in Christ.

Come to your work from your personal prayer;
your public prayer with the community depends on this.
Come to the liturgy steeped in the scriptures of the day
lest your presidency be illiterate.
Come to the place of prayer early,
enter freely and peacefully upon that holy ground
lest your ministry be hasty or unprepared.
Come to your ministry as do all God's people:
deeply aware of your need for the Lord's mercy.

Depend on and allow the other ministers
to offer their services
as they have been called to do.
Let them be your fellow ministers,
not personal aides or underlings.

Be gentle when correction is needed.
Remember that the liturgy is the assembly's prayer;
because you are one with them, it is yours too.
Call your fellow ministers
to faithfulness and preparedness
by the model of your own work.
Ask not of others
what you do not demand of yourself.

Let every prayer and word you speak
from chair, ambo and table
be clear, strong and true.
Trust always in the Spirit,
but not too much in your own spontaneity.
Anyone can read texts;
only the believer can pray them.
Pray the prayers and proclaim the scriptures!
Let all your movement and gesture
be strong, graceful and with purpose;
the hurried step is distracting,
and the weak gesture insignificant.
Let nothing be affected;
let everything be done with reverence.
Handle holy things with holy care.

Let your ministry be emptied of self-interest.
Remember that it is the assembly's prayer that you serve.
Think of yourself not as the center of things
but as the one who helps keep things
centered on the Lord.
Let your eyes fall often on God's people
as the eyes of the servant
are on the hands of the master.
Minister according to the customs of the church,
and not by personal taste;
this prayer belongs to the people,
and they trust it to your care.

Let the liturgy be your prayer
lest the celebration space become your stage.

When your brothers and sisters
praise and thank you for your work,
delight in the rite that has become their prayer
and rejoice in the work
the Lord has accomplished through you.
Be faithful in the work you do,
for through it the Lord saves his people.

THE MINISTRY OF LECTORS

Yours is a share
in the work of the Lord's Spirit
who opens our hearts to God's holy word.
Yours is the task
of telling our family story, the story of salvation.
Yours is to proclaim the true and saving word of God.
You are the messenger of God's love for us.
Your task is to proclaim a word
that challenges, confronts and captures our hearts.
You proclaim a word that heals and comforts and consoles.
Yours is the ministry of the table of God's word,
which feeds the hunger and the longing
of our hearts for truth.
Yours is to offer the story
of the "great things the Lord has done for us"
that we might turn to the table of eucharist
with good cause to give thanks and praise.
Yours is nothing less
than the ministry of the Lord's voice
calling out in the midst of God's people.

Come to your work from your personal prayer,
praying that the Spirit will open your heart
to what you proclaim.
Prepare the word which is yours to speak:
Study the scriptures, understand the passage,
let it dwell deep within you.
Come to your work
in awesome reverence of the word you proclaim:
It is the Lord's word.
Come to your ministry
as one judged and saved by the word you speak.
Anyone can read the scriptures in public;
only the believer can proclaim them.

Approach the ambo,
the table of the Lord's word,
as you would the Lord himself:
with reverence and awe.
Handle the book of the Lord's word
with great care:
It is a tabernacle of the Lord's presence.
Let your eyes fall often
on the faces of the assembly:
They are the body of the Lord
whose word you proclaim.
Let the Lord's peace settle in your heart,
that your voice may be clear and steady.
Let your voice echo the sound of the word
with conviction,
with gentleness,
with strength,
and with wonder.
Remember that the story you tell
is filled with a drama you need not supply
but must always convey.

Like the prophet,
you will sometimes proclaim
what no one wants to hear;
remember always your own need
to hear the hard saying
and never imagine that your ministry
places you above what you proclaim.
If you are the best of the parish lectors,
be gentle in helping others to improve.
If you are the least of the parish lectors,
seek out that help which others can give.
If you do not know how well you read — ask:
Be grateful for constructive criticism
and humbled by any praise your receive.
Every lector wants to read at the Easter Vigil

but not all will be assigned:
Be patient in waiting your turn
and be nourished by the word that others proclaim.
Let no minister of the word
think that there is nothing left to learn:
another commentary and another workshop
cannot but help the open mind and heart.

When your brothers and sisters
praise and thank you for your work,
take delight in the word they have heard
and rejoice in the work
the Lord has accomplished through you.
Be faithful in the work you do,
for through it the Lord saves his people.

THE MINISTRY OF DEACONS

Yours is a share
in the work of the Lord's Spirit
who calls the whole church
to the *diakonia* of the liturgy,
of the word and of charity.
Yours is the task
of preparing the Lord's table
for the prayer of the assembly,
for the communion
of God's people.

Yours is the work of proclaiming the gospel
and preaching it
in season and out of season,
announcing the word of challenge and comfort
that all need to hear.
Yours is the ministry of charity
to those who are in need,
especially Christ's beloved,
the poorest of the poor.

Your hands guide the newly baptized
through the dying and rising of Christ
in the saving waters of the pool and font.
You stand as witness for the church
as a man and woman
bind their lives together
in Christ,
in love,
in fidelity,
in marriage.

Come to your work from your personal prayer;
your public prayer with the church
depends on this.

Come to the liturgy
steeped in the scriptures of the day
lest your preaching be illiterate.
Come to the place of prayer early;
enter freely and peacefully
upon that holy ground
lest your ministry be hasty or unprepared.
Come to your ministry as do all God's people:
deeply aware of your need
for the Lord's mercy.

Depend on the other ministers
and allow them to offer their services
as they have been called to do.

Let every prayer and word you speak
from chair, ambo and table
be clear, strong and true.
Anyone can read texts;
only the believer can proclaim them.
Pray the prayers
and proclaim the scripture!

Let your movement and gesture
be strong, graceful and with purpose;
the hurried step is distracting,
the weak gesture insignificant.
Let nothing be affected;
let everything be done with reverence.
Handle holy things with holy care.
Let your ministry
be emptied of self-interest.

Let your eyes fall often on God's people
as the eyes of the servant
are on the hands of the master.

When your brothers and sisters
praise and thank you for your work,
delight in the word they have heard,
and rejoice in the work
the Lord has accomplished through you.
Be faithful in the work you do,
for through it the Lord saves his people.

THE MINISTRY OF PREACHING

Yours is a share
in the work of the Lord's Spirit
who opens our hearts
to the Good News of salvation.
Yours is the ministry of the table of God's word.
Yours is the work of breaking open the scriptures
that God's people might be nourished
by the food of the Lord's word.
Yours is the ministry of Jesus
who came to announce
that the reign of God is at hand.
Yours is the voice which opens
the challenge and the consolation of the gospel
in the parables of your homily.
Yours is to tell a story
that tells the story of God's love for us.
Yours is the prophet's ministry
among the home town people.
Yours is the task of announcing
promise when hope is gone,
love when it has cooled,
justice to the oppressed and the oppressors,
joy when tears run freely,
and God when we are less than human.

Come to your work from your personal prayer,
come filled with the word
that judges and saves your own life.
Bear the book of the gospels
as the weight of God's judgment
and the breadth of God's mercy.
Bear this book as the ark of the covenant,
with reverence, awe and wonder.
Proclaim the gospel as if our lives depended on it:
They do.

Proclaim the Good News as though we had never heard it:
We are slow to understand.
Prepare your proclamation of the gospel
as carefully as you prepare your homily:
The one will never fail;
the other may be forgotten.
Come to your preaching
mindful of your own need
to hear the gospel message:
When you do this, your word is clear and true.

Preach the gospel:
This is all we need to hear.
Pray for God's Spirit
that your mind and heart be enlightened
by the light of Christ.
Let your preaching speak to this age,
but not be conformed to it;
let your thoughts be transformed
by the renewal of your mind in Christ Jesus,
and we shall be re-created.
Preach to us as people you have come to know;
we know you so well by what you preach.
Struggle as you must
when preaching the difficult text or the hard saying:
Your honest struggle helps us in our own.
Spare us the used homily
when the cycle comes around again;
our lives have changed
(as has your own),
and we hunger for fresh food
from the gospel table.
When the Lord has been sparing of inspiration,
be brief:
We will understand.

Let not even your own sin
hold back from us the gospel's demands.

Preach the word in season and out of season.
Do not shrink from naming what is sinful;
how else will we know our need for salvation?
Preach sin and grace
for this is what we know the best
and need to hear again.
Preach the reign of God in our midst:
Help us to know its signs and presence.
Tell us the story of God's mercy:
No other story does as much.
Show us Jesus dying and rising among us:
This is what we have came here to see.

When your brothers and sisters
praise and thank you for your work,
take delight in the word that has nourished them
and rejoice in the work
the Lord has accomplished through you.
Be faithful in the work you do,
for through it the Lord saves his people.

THE MINISTRY OF CATECHISTS
OF CHRISTIAN INITIATION

Yours is a share
in the work of the Lord's Spirit
who calls women, men and children
to faith and to communion with the church,
the assembly of believers, the body of Christ.
Yours is the task of echoing
the voice of God, who speaks and calls with love
in the hearts and minds
of inquirers, catechumens and the elect.
Yours is the warm welcome
that opens hearts to the Lord's story in the scripture,
to his presence in prayer,
to the promise of his gift in the eucharist.
Yours is the hand that helps newcomers
steady their steps along the road of faith's journey,
along the path of God's love,
along the way of the cross.
Yours is the companionship
that shines in the darkness of doubt,
that strengthens the heart that is weary,
and waits through the worries of fear.
You are the brother, the sister in Christ
who helps our newcomers
to know Christ as brother, as Lord, as Savior.

Come to your work
from your personal prayer,
the wellspring from which your faith is refreshed.
Come to your ministry
with your heart open to all the ways
the Lord may move, shape, mold and form you
as an icon of his presence for the catechumens.
Immerse yourself in the scriptures
of the Lord's story
so that his story becomes yours

and you become his.
Grow in your love of Jesus
and ask for the grace to share
the story of his love for you
with those you teach and sponsor.
Be patient with the questions, fears and anxiety
of those who seek to know the Lord
and to follow him.
Invite the catechumens to pray with you,
invite them to share the story of their journey,
their story of faith.
Be there for them
as the Lord is there for you:
fully, freely, and with forgiveness.
At the Sunday dismissal,
cherish the word proclaimed
and the eucharist you share,
and pray for that day when all will be one
in the sacrament of the Lord's table.

When the catechumens
praise and thank you for your work,
delight in the faith you share with them
and rejoice in the work
the Lord has accomplished through you.
Be faithful in the work you do,
for through it the Lord saves his people.

THE MINISTRY OF DANCED PRAYER

Yours is a share
in the work of the Lord's Spirit
who is ever moving
in our hearts and among God's people.
You gesture with your whole self
the prayer we know in our hearts:
With us and for us
you bring that prayer to living sign;
yours is a ministry of word become flesh.
You move among us like God's own Spirit:
with beauty and strength,
with fire and peace,
with tenderness and power.
In all of this you lead us,
in the Spirit,
to lift our hands and hearts
in praise of the living God.

Come to your work from your personal prayer.
Come filled with the song,
the word,
and the silence of your prayer.
Let the dance of your own prayer
overflow in prayer and movement
for the assembled believers.
Please, do not come to dance for us;
come only to lead us in prayer
through the dance that is your prayer.
Prepare for your ministry
as the preacher prepares for the homily:
with time, energy, prayer and work.
We are not interested in extemporaneous performance;
dance for us and with us
the prayer you know by heart.

Understand
that we will not always understand
your ministry.
Be patient with us,
and help us to learn,
to appreciate the wonder
of all the gifts the Lord shares
through our brothers and sisters.
Teach us to pray with our whole selves,
and be patient with us
when we are awkward and embarrassed.
Be gentle in leading us and our prayer,
and the heart and flesh from which we pray.
Remember that your ministry
is a giving of self
and that your danced prayer
is a unique giving of your whole self
in the Lord's service.
More than most ministers,
you render your whole person and prayer
vulnerable to critique and misunderstanding.
Forgive us where we sin;
forgive our jealousy and pettiness.
Do not wonder if we enjoyed your dance;
rather, ponder how it has (or hasn't)
led us to pray with you.

When your brothers and sisters
praise and thank you for your work,
take delight in the prayer they have shared,
and be thankful for the work
the Lord has accomplished through your gift.
Be faithful in the work you do,
for through it the Lord saves his people.

THE MINISTRY
OF EUCHARISTIC MINISTERS

Yours is a share
in the work of the Lord's Spirit
who makes of us
one bread, one body,
the cup of blessing which we bless.
Yours is the work
of ministering Christ's body and blood
to the body of Christ, the church.
Yours is service at the Lord's reconciling table.
You name for each of us
the gifts we have offered
and the gifts we receive:
"The Body of Christ, the Blood of Christ."
You minister holy food to holy people
in the holiest of all communions.
Yours is the ministry of the One
who was broken and poured out for our sake:
the ministry of Christ
who is our Passover
and our lasting peace.

Come to your work from your personal prayer,
praying that the Lord will heal your brokenness
as you break and pour out yourselves for others.
Remember the purity of the gifts you minister
and how great is your need for the Lord's mercy.
Learn to love the eucharist you minister:
Let it heal the hurt your heart is slow to acknowledge;
let it make you one with all that is living;
let it help you revere all those whom you serve.
Ministers of the eucharist are many;
truly eucharistic ministers
are what you must become.
Let your service at the Lord's table
make of your life

a table of mercy and welcome
for all you know and meet.

In and outside the worship space,
reverence those you serve
as you would reverence the sacrament you minister.
When you minister to friends and family,
remember that the greatest bond you share is in the Lord.
When you minister to visitors and strangers,
reverence them as you would your closest friend.
When you minister to those with whom you are at odds,
reverence them as the Lord does you in your sin.
Some will esteem you as "holy"
because of the work you do:
Remember that your holiness
is the Lord's work within you.
When you are asked to serve at inconvenient times,
let the needs of God's people
be your first consideration.
When you begin to think that your ministry
makes you an important person in the community,
remember that what the Lord did at table
became a sign of the cross.

When your brothers and sisters
praise and thank you for your work,
take delight in the communion
you share with them in Christ
and rejoice in the work
the Lord has accomplished through you.
Be faithful in the work you do,
for through it the Lord saves his people.

ONE BREAD, ONE CUP,
ONE MINISTRY

There is much overlapping in the reflections we have offered.
This is to be expected when we are speaking of one ministry
(the Lord's) and of one spirituality (rooted in our baptism).
Our reflections also all reveal some specificity precisely because
the gifts and ministries are many. This is not to say that they
compete with one another; rather they complement and serve
one another as they serve God's people at prayer. In a kitchen,
the one who washes the dishes receives less public attention
than does the one who prepares the meal. Still, without the
scullery help the chef's creations will never make it to the table.
The service of both contributes to the nourishment of the din-
ers, and when either is absent, the people go hungry. It is much
the same at the Lord's table and among those who serve that
table. Value, esteem and importance are determined not by the
particular service rendered, but by the Lord's service in which
we have shared and through which God's people are served
and saved.

In a previous chapter we noted the anomalous situation
in which the servants at the Lord's table receive top billing and
front-row seats. Although such attention may lead to misunderstanding, it is also appropriate. This is so, not because
those who serve merit attention to themselves, but because
the service they render is revealing of Christ's service in our
midst. It is beneficial to the assembly to know that the baptismal
impulse to imitate and incarnate the Lord's work is alive and
flourishing in their midst. This notion will be clearly understood in the community whose ministers first recognize it themselves. As the community begins to name the ministry of
lectors, presiders, and musicians as the Lord's ministry, it will
begin to name its own assembled self as the body of Christ.
The church, Christ's body, is the Lord's ministry in the building
up of the city of God. The new Jerusalem is as near or far
away as the local church community is to enfleshing the dying
and rising of Jesus who is its Sovereign.

The liturgy is not a theater where actors on stage take bows and applause at curtain call. It is an arena of holy ground where God's people stand naked and empty-handed in the Creator's presence. Our time and prayer in this holy place are served by sinners like ourselves whose only vesture is ours, too: We are all clothed in Christ as the new creation. These servants point the way for all who assemble. Their proximity to table and ambo is one of service, not priority. These servants are seen and heard so that all might see and hear the Lord among us. If they are the first to be served from the table, it is so they might be nourished for the serving of others. They are distinguished not so much by what they do, but by whose work they have become in its doing.

As we began, we shall conclude these reflections with the words of Saint Paul:

> I therefore, the prisoner in the Lord, beg you to lead a life worthy of the calling to which you have been called, with all humility and gentleness, with patience, bearing with one another in love, making every effort to maintain the unity of the Spirit in the bond of peace. There is one body and one Spirit, just as you were called to the one hope of your calling, one Lord, one faith, one baptism, one God and Father of all, who is above all and through all and in all. . . . You were taught to put away your former way of life, your old self, corrupt and deluded by its lusts, and to be renewed in the spirit of your minds, and to clothe yourselves with the new self, created according to the likeness of God in true righteousness and holiness.
>
> (Ephesians 4:1–6, 22–24)

Notes

1. See *Environment and Art in Catholic Worship,* 28.
2. *Music in Catholic Worship,* 23.
3. *Constitution on the Sacred Liturgy,* 83.

Chapter 8

BLESSING *and* DISMISSAL

There is a certain wisdom in our ritual for celebrating the eucharist that should not escape our attention: The best of opening rites[1] bring us with no delay to the table of God's word. Almost as soon as we have gathered, we begin to tell the family's story. The stories within this story are many, as they are in every family. These are stories of beginnings and roots, of life and of death, of hard times and how we survived them. Most of all, this is the story of that binding and merciful Lover who makes us one as family. Because this is the story of God's love for us, it is promise as well as history, and so it is the story of our future.

The story told and shared, we go to the family table that is ours because it is the Lord's. There is no denying that we come to this table to feast, but first we offer that greatest blessing before a meal: the praise and thanks of the eucharistic prayer. With one great "Amen!" we share the Lord's supper. The family gathering is now complete in the Passover meal of the new covenant.

Finally, and with a brevity the opening rite would do well to imitate, we pray for the Lord's blessing upon us, and are dismissed for the work we have been nourished to do. There is a wonderful economy of time here that provides for the elements of our prayer just what is appropriate. In similar fashion, this discussion is concluded by a few pages of "blessing and dismissal."

BLESSING

An old Latin blessing before meals begins with the words, *"Benedicamus Domino!"* or "Let us bless the Lord!" We are perhaps more accustomed to blessing meals, food and a variety of other items than to blessing God. The blessing best known to all of us is the gesture of blessing ourselves with the sign of the cross. The words that accompany this simple action tell us much about the nature of blessing. "In the name of the Father, and of the Son, and of the Holy Spirit. Amen." Whatever might prompt us to make this gestured invocation, its accompanying words turn our hearts' and minds' attention to the God who made, redeemed and sustains us. This is true blessing at its best. When we bless persons or objects, our prayer should be one of thanksgiving to God for the gift of this person or object, which thanksgiving prompts us to call God "holy" for all we have received.[2]

We review this understanding of blessing by way of summary and parting admonition.

Back to Basics

From our initial discussion of those basic questions, "Whom do we worship? Why do we worship? How do we worship whom we worship?" we have looked at liturgy (in particular, the eucharist) as one great blessing of God by the assembly of God's people. Liturgy is a benediction in which we "speak well" (*bene* + *dicere*) of the mighty and merciful God whose people we are. Christian worship is the way in which the community of believers is "signed by the cross" while proclaiming the blessed Trinity revealed in the gospel.

Jesus at the Center

Because we stand as those in the world who bless the Lord, we have come to see the vital importance of being prepared to stand in the sanctuary of blessing that the liturgy is: Any other approach is deemed criminal in the halls of kingdom justice. We have made distinctions between formal and informal, creative and contemporary worship. We have seen that the truest blessing we speak is the one conformed to the dying and rising of Jesus; that the most honest blessing we make is the one faithful to the heritage of blessing that is ours in the Anointed One of Israel, and the one faithful to the Risen One in our own experience and times. Overall, we have said that blessing in the sanctuary of worship is validated in Christ and by our share in the work of justice accomplished in his paschal mystery.

Finally, we have seen that the ministry of blessing God belongs to the whole assembly by virtue of their baptism; spiritualities and particular expressions of various ministries are all one, rooted in, branded and healed by the cross of Christ. We have asked those in each of these ministries to reflect on the service they offer as a share in the Lord's saving ministry on behalf of God's people.

In all of this, the God-centeredness of our worship and life in and outside the sanctuary is of preeminent importance. A reading of the signs of our times suggests that reminding ourselves of this is of particular value for those who worship in the church in North America. We Christians are those who walk the path of Jesus, whose meshing of humanity and divinity is our salvation. If in these pages I have erred on the side of divinity, it has not been without cause; be assured that in my personal life I tend to err in the opposite direction.

DISMISSAL

Our parting admonition is a simple one: Let the reading of this book be an occasion for appreciating more deeply our celebration of God's mercy in the liturgy. Do not let these pages become a tool for judging others, their prayer and how they offer it. It is my hope that those who read this book will read it in terms of their own and others' liturgy. My fear, however, is that they will then run back to their parishes' liturgy teams, presiders, ministers and chairpersons to criticize the community's prayer. Before this book is put down, remember there is little new in these pages; at best we have rehearsed a theology, spirituality and liturgy as old as that upper room that Peter and John prepared for Christ's Passover.

Anything here that seems to be new is only apparently so. What may strike the individual as discovery may well be "old hat" to those whose ministry and liturgy these pages may lead you to criticize. Keep in mind that in many ways our communities have been faithful in the task of doing what Christ has commanded. In those areas where we have been less than faithful there is work to be done, but this work will not be so much accomplished by change in liturgical style or practice as it will be realized in the deepening conversion of the hearts of all of us. That conversion, it should be no surprise, is the Lord's work in our lives.

Patience and Understanding

This is not said to stifle zeal, enthusiasm or renewal among those whose ministry attends to divine service. Rather it is intended to temper zeal with patience, to infuse enthusiasm with gentleness and to bless renewal efforts with a holy and wholesome respect for the prayer that God's people already offer. In this we can learn from our recent past. The turmoil in our church's life occasioned by the nearly overnight reforms of the 1960s are a part of worship history we would do well not to repeat. The reforms, in many cases, presumed an expression of faith experience whose vocabulary was perhaps more foreign to us than the Latin about to meet its demise. Patience, understanding and catechesis should have been the order of the day, and must be in our own times as the liturgy continues to be renewed by our study, understanding and experience, and as we prepare for a new generation of liturgical books. As those who usually err on the side of our humanity, we must make the effort to see that our work, our prayer and the service we offer are one with Christ Jesus, the Lord, whose canticle of praise in the halls of heaven is ours in every age.

Rejoice in the Lord always; Again I will say, Rejoice. Let your gentleness be known to everyone. The Lord is near. Do not worry about anything, but in everything by prayer and supplication with thanksgiving let your requests be made known to God. And the peace of God, which surpasses all understanding, will guard your hearts and minds in Christ Jesus. Finally, beloved, whatever is true, whatever is honorable, whatever is just, whatever is pure, whatever is pleasing, whatever is commendable, if there is any excellence and if there is anything worthy of praise, think about these things. Keep on doing the things that you have learned and received and heard and seen in me, and the God of peace will be with you.

(Philippians 4:4–9)

Notes

1. The best of opening rites is not cluttered by the inclusion of several disparate elements; it brings us together and prepares us for hearing the word proclaimed.

2. This is the kind of prayer that Mary speaks in her canticle of blessing, the Magnificat (Luke 1:46–55). Our eucharistic prayers also reflect this "blessing" dynamic that has its roots in the *berekah* (blessing) prayers of our Jewish ancestry.